'No other novelist among us today has quite his philosophical weight, intellectual force, or spiritual understanding, and few would risk what Mr Johnson has here: to tell a new kind of story entirely, unlike anything before it. *Dreamer* is an inspired and glorious achievement, infused with its author's expansive wisdom, his vibrant historical and moral imagination, and most of all, his heart . . . This is a book to sustain us – black and white, all of us – and so powerfully wrought as to endure in our literature so long as our literature itself endures. I am humbled by *Dreamer* and grateful for it. It is a transcendent, brilliant book.' David Guterson, author of *Snow Falling on Cedars*

'Charles Johnson's *Dreamer* is a beautiful and heartfelt novel of substance; intriguing and cleverly rendered, it has a plot that entertains even as it throws a light on the life of Martin Luther King during that epoch of America's struggles with civil rights.' Oscar Hijuelos, author of *The Mambo Kings Play Songs of Love*, Winner of the Pulitzer Prize

'Compelling and profound, *Dreamer* is a book fully equal to its monumental subject, Martin Luther King Jr. Charles Johnson is one of the treasures of modern American literature.' Robert Olen Butler, author of *A Good Scent from a Strange Mountain*, Winner of the Pulitzer Prize

'[Johnson's] new novel . . . takes bold, creative risks, bringing off many unlikely feats . . . It's a joy to read fiction in which there is a cultivated vision at work.'   *New York Times Books Review*

'Johnson is a superb craftsman . . . It is a measure of the rich profundity of *Dreamer* that its title could refer to any number of people: King himself, the narrator, the writer. As I closed the book, I rather hoped it referred to the reader.'   *Sunday Telegraph*

'Like a skiff exploring history's more hidden currents, Johnson's poetic language drifts with care over the moiling currents of King's intellect, leaving in its wake a wonderful, prismatic novel, exhorting and testifying, but never preaching.'   *Guardian*

'Elegant, erudite and fearless.'   *Time Out*

'Superbly told, fictionalised history is rarely so good.'   *The Times*

'Johnson is interested in big ideas, both political and philosophical, and he works them neatly into a gripping storyline.'   *Scotland on Sunday*

'[A] finely imagined novel.'   *Sunday Telegraph*

'In his brilliant challenging new nov
credible rendering – a worthy success

GW00502070

a rewarding book that will provoke careful thought about how we have succeeded and failed in our quest to ensure equality.'   *Chicago Tribune*

'*Dreamer* is what we've come to expect from Johnson: a tale that's complex, richly told and open-ended enough to inspire readers to launch their own imaginative explorations.'   *Washington Post Book World*

'A remarkable tale . . . a brilliant historical novel.'   *Publishing News*

'After reading this novel, we think it scandalous that this brilliant American author does not have a wider readership in the UK . . . [*Dreamer*] vividly conjures the social unrest and sense of possibility of the age.'

Good Book Guide

'A wonderful novel. Guaranteed to make you cry.'   *Elle Magazine*

'Johnson weaves a subtle and playful narrative . . . the most remarkable creative response to its subject since Berio's *O King*.'   *Independent*

'His fiction transcends the immediate concerns of race and colour, and will find its place in the great body of literature produced by America's humanitarian tradition.'   *Literary Review*

'Sad, sophisticated, powerful stuff from a top black American writer.'

Mail on Sunday

'A masterful portrait . . . At times, the tone of the book is like that of King himself; nothing short of visionary and inspiring.'   *The Latest*

'What unites *Dreamer*'s diverse concerns – biography, politics, sociology, ethics – is its passionate desire to celebrate black history and to vindicate King . . . it is powerful as a moral tribute.'   *The Sunday Times*

'A fascinating consideration of the gap between image and substance and the appalling human price paid when moral authority challenges brute political power.'   *New Internationalist*

DREAMER

Charles Johnson

CANONGATE

First published in Great Britain in 1998 by Canongate Books Ltd,
14 High Street, Edinburgh, EH1 1TE

First paperback edition published in 2000

This edition published in 2004

10 9 8 7 6 5 4 3 2 1

British Library Cataloguing-in-Publication Data
A catalogue record for this book is available on
request from the British Library.

ISBN 1 84195 490 X

Printed and bound by
Cox & Wyman Ltd, Reading, Berkshire

www.canongate.net

To the memory of Lee Goerner

ACKNOWLEDGMENTS

Acknowledgment is gratefully made to the books and people without whom this novel could not have been written. Of special importance are Stephen B. Oates's superb *Let the Trumpet Sound*, David L. Lewis's *King: A Critical Biography*, Lerone Bennett Jr.'s *What Manner of Man*, Coretta Scott King's *My Life with Martin Luther King, Jr.*, James H. Cone's *Martin & Malcolm & America*, John J. Ansbro's *Martin Luther King, Jr.: The Making of a Mind*, Keith D. Miller's *Voice of Deliverance*, David Garrow's three-volume *Martin Luther King, Jr. and the Civil Rights Movement*, Mark Lane's *Code Name Zorro*, James Earl Ray's *Who Killed Martin Luther King?*, John A. Williams's *The King God Didn't Save*, Julius Lester's *Search for the New Land*, Noel Leo Erskine's *King Among the Theologians*, volumes 1 and 2 of *The Papers of Martin Luther King, Jr.*, and James R. Ralph Jr.'s "Home Truths: Dr. King and the Chicago Freedom Movement" (*American Visions*, Aug./Sept. 1994).

I must also acknowledge my indebtedness to my agent, Anne Borchardt, for her brilliant advice; Dr. Rudolph Byrd for taking me to King's birth home; poet Sharon Bryan for accompanying me to the King Memorial at the Lorraine Motel; Joyce Carol Oates for providing the Henry Adams definition of politics; Dr. Ricardo J. Quinones for placing in my hands a copy of his invaluable book, *The Changes of Cain*; Eknath Easwaran for his voluminous writings on the life of the spirit; to Guy Murchie's *The Seven Mysteries of Life*; philosopher Scott Kramer for helping me remember the '6os; poet Ethelbert Miller and filmmaker Jon Dichter for spiritual support; Gray Cassidy for his martial-arts expertise; Janie Smith for her hours spent typing the manuscript; and my wife, Joan, for her bottomless knowledge about the Book.

DREAMER

"The Pauper has to die before the Prince can be born."

MEISTER ECKHART

"But unto Cain and to his offering the Lord had not respect. And Cain was very wroth, and his countenance fell."

GENESIS 4:5

"If you sow the seeds of violence in your struggle, unborn generations will reap the whirlwind of social disintegration."

MARTIN LUTHER KING JR., *Strength to Love*

"Behold, this dreamer cometh. Come now therefore, and let us slay him, and cast him into one of the pits, and we will say: Some evil beast hath devoured him; and we shall see what will become of his dreams."

GENESIS 37:19–20

PROLOGUE

In the Upsouth cities he visited, violence followed him like a biblical curse, but one step ahead of his assassins. Despite his clerical vows, or perhaps because of them (I am come to send fire on the earth, Luke 12:49), he walked through a world aflame. Chicago in the hundred-degree summer heat of 1966 was the site for the special form of crisis his wing of the Movement produced: families divided, fathers at the throats of their sons, brothers spilling each other's blood. Unhappily, I have the eloquence of neither Guido the Angelic nor Teresa of Avila, and so with each halting sentence I pray for the words to demonstrate how this was the beginning of his northern crusade to undo the work of the Devil. This was the battlefield, a modern plain of Kurukshetra, where in the midst of a shooting war between Richard Daley's police and black snipers on the West Side (two were dead, hundreds were in detention), he

*composed that electrifying speech, "A Knock at Midnight,"
read for him by friends at St. Peter's Cathedral, seeing how he
was stretched so thin, there in Chicago, that he couldn't fly as
scheduled to Geneva and instead spent three hellish nights
rushing from one burning slum to another, pleading until 4
A.M. with both armed camps for peace.* It is . . . midnight in
our world, and the darkness is so deep that we can hardly see
which way to turn.

*He was tired by the time the Movement reached the
North. His life had always belonged to others. For ten years
he'd been God's athlete, traveling nearly eight million miles
(one-fourth the distance to Mars) back and forth across a
country as divided as it had been during the Civil War, giving
thousands of speeches in churches where he was celebrated as
the heir of Thoreau—or better as the North American
mahatma (Great Soul), meeting with presidents and heads of
state, performing more eulogies for the Movement's martyrs
than he cared to remember, leading his generals in the siege of
one southern town after another; flying to Africa, then to
India, and five years before to Oslo to accept the Nobel Peace
Prize with a team of federal agents right on his heels, as they
always were, closer even than his own heartbeat, he sometimes
felt, though you had to wonder where they were and what the
devil they were doing when that Harlem madwoman, Izola
Curry, plunged a Japanese letter opener into his chest. Or
when his Montgomery home was bombed, nearly killing his
young wife and baby Yolanda.*

*More tired, acclaimed, hated, gaoled, and hunted than
any other Negro in history, but living this close to death was as
inevitable as his being ordained a minister when he was eigh-
teen. No matter how he looked at it, his calling meant that
from the moment he donned his robe the laws governing his
life were different from those of the vast majority of men;
indeed, it was no longer his life to do with as he pleased. The*

14

world owned him long before he could own himself. As it is with candles, so it was with him: the more light he gave, the less there was of him. Moreover, since the First World War the Army had sniffed something dangerous in his family, some blood-gift for subversion more radical than anything Lenin dreamed up in Moscow; they had watched his father and grandfather closely, and interfered with their lives just as they did his, as devoted to shaming him, discrediting him, and driving him from public life as he was to bringing his ever expanding congregation a bit closer to the Kingdom of God on earth. People always thought he was older than his thirty-seven years. In point of fact, he felt old. Centuries old, and looked over fifty in some photographs: washed by all waters. Sometimes late at night, when he couldn't sleep before yet another early morning flight, and his leather suitcase from Paris lay packed on the table in yet another unfamiliar hotel room, and the memories came washing over him in waves—the poor living like chattel, children dynamited in a church, Watts burning for six days, the death threats spewing through the telephone at his wife—on those nights he wept for the blood spilled by his enemies, for his own life's lost options, for the outrageous fragility of what he hoped to achieve in a world smothering in materialism, in the propaganda of sensation, in scientific marvels unmoored from any sense of morality, and he wondered, there in the darkness before the dawn of what might be his last day on earth, if he'd ever been young at all.

"Don't go to Chicago," his closest advisor said. "You can't win there. You don't know cities. Stay on your own turf."

The enemy was more elusive, said Hosea Williams and the city's famed pastor, Joseph H. Jackson. Not crude country sheriffs like "Bull" Connor, who fell tail over tin cup before the world's cameras into the bully-buffoon role they scripted for him, or heavy-browed bigots like George Wallace, whose reactions made outstanding copy for the cause. In Chicago, the vil-

lains were faceless institutions: banks, real estate agents, insurance companies, and landlords hardly better off, in some cases, than their ghetto tenants. But this town, he knew, was the Up North equivalent of Birmingham. If they could triumph here, establishing a beachhead for satyagraha (truth force) in a brutal city with a murder rate of slightly more than two people per day, here in balkanized ethnic enclaves that spawned Al Capone and hardened street gangs like the Cobras, the Vice Lords, and the Black Stone Rangers, here in a city where Stokely Carmichael's poorly timed but inevitable cry for Black Power during their Mississippi march to support one of the South's wounded heroes, James Meredith, opened a Pandora's box of rage and rang deeper into black hearts than any appeal for love (he knew betrayal, a stab in the back when he saw it, but told Carmichael, "I've been used before"), then they could conquer any citadel of inequality in the world.

Yet no one thought he could win.

A decade after his Montgomery victory, and spiraling successes throughout the South, nigh Hegelian in the mysterious way the Movement kept changing as he chased it, and changing him, pushing him higher and higher, beyond anything he'd dreamed possible in college, from local bus boycotts to unqualified calls for integration, and finally to grander dreams of global peace and equality—a decade after his finest triumphs for nonviolence, the press, and even people who'd joined hands with him singing "We Shall Overcome," now saw his methods as outmoded, his insistence on loving one's enemies as lunacy, his opposition to Black Power as outright betrayal. Oh, he needed a victory here. The Chicago crusade was costing as much as $10,000 some months. In the spirit of Martin Luther four centuries earlier, he taped his demands for the poor on the door of City Hall after marching three miles with five thousand men and women of goodwill from Soldier Field; but despite money spent and speeches delivered, the mayor's office maneu-

vered, matching his call for jobs and open housing with promises and claims for progress that his critics dismissed as smoke and mirrors, mere Band-Aids aimed at making the problem (and him) go away. Never a day passed when he did not read that his stature was diminished, his day of leadership done, and he could not ignore his critics if he was, as he so often claimed, committed to the truth. Twelve times he'd been imprisoned in Alabama and Georgia jails, stabbed once, spat upon, and targeted for death so many times he could say, like the Apostle Paul, "I bear in my body the marks of the Lord." Yet for all his sojourning on the Jericho Road, his long journey through the valley of the shadow of death, his deeper, esoteric message about freedom had barely been heard. The gleaming keys he offered to the Kingdom made men and women who accepted his exoteric, surface-skimming political speeches shrink back once they saw the long-sealed door he was asking them to enter; they could not pass through that portal and remain as they were: white and black, male and female, Jew and Gentile, rich and poor—these were ephemeral garments, he knew, and could no more clear that entrance than a camel through a needle's eye. To gain the dizzying heights of the mountaintop the self's baggage had to be abandoned in the valley. Little wonder, then, that so few grasped the goal he pointed to, or that on the Mississippi march and then in Chicago he was booed, and would have wept over this but instead thought back with thanksgiving (and was not all thought, as Heidegger pointed out, a form of thanksgiving?) to his professor at Morehouse, Benjamin Mays, who impressed upon him the importance of learning Henley's poem "Invictus" (It matters not how strait the gate . . .). *After his twelve years of sacrifice, the young people in the Mississippi crowd called him a traitor, an Uncle Tom* (How charged with punishments the scroll . . .). *In the cities, they sang "We Shall Over-Run."* (I am the master of my fate: / I am the captain of my soul.)

But somehow their rejection and resistance to his vision fit well into the way he then understood the world. He was a tightrope walker straddling two worlds. One of matter. One of spirit. Every social evil he could think of, and every "ontological fear," as he was fond of saying lately, arose from that mysterious dichotomy inscribed at the heart of things: self and other, I and Thou, inner and outer, perceiver and perceived. It was a schism that, if not healed, would consume the entire world. Martyrdom held no appeal for him, but for every sorcerer named Jesus there was a Judas; for every bodhisattva called Gandhi, a Poona Brahmin named Nathuram Godse. The way to the crown was, now and forever, the cross. And it made no sense to carry the cross unless one was prepared to be crucified.

He sensed how close he was to the end, this Christian boy from Atlanta, this product of three generations of black preachers, this theistic idealist, and sometimes he wished he was two people, or perhaps three. One to co-pastor each Sunday beside his father at Ebenezer Baptist Church. Another to spend more time with his family, especially with his children; catch up on his reading (especially Tillich, Fromm, and Buber, who interested him more now than when he was in college); listen to opera, take his wife dancing, play basketball with the Southern Christian Leadership Council's staff, leave his blue suits in the closet, dress more casually, and perhaps one day pursue a simple, ascetic life similar to that of Thich Nhat Hanh, the poet, Zen master, and chairman of the Vietnamese peace delegation whom he was currently promoting as a candidate for the Nobel. As he'd told his Montgomery congregation the day he resigned as pastor in 1959, he longed to escape "the strain of being known . . . I've been faced with the responsibility of trying to do as one man what five or six people ought to be doing . . . What I have been doing is giving, giving, giving, and not stopping to retreat and meditate like I should—to come back. If the situation is not changed, I will be a physical and emotional wreck. I have to reorganize my personality and reorient my life. I have been too long in the crowd, too long in the forest . . ."

And a third person to direct the Chicago campaign from the foul-smelling flat the SCLC and the Coordinating Council of Community Organizations leased at 1550 South Hamlin Street in the heart of "Slumdale." From a security standpoint its location was a nightmare. The neighborhood was notorious for crime. Saturday-night shootings and streetwalkers. Establishing a perimeter was impossible. Any rooftop across the street would tempt a rifleman. Noises from downstairs, loud, braying conversations from other apartments, could not be kept out. When a sanitation truck rolled by, the floor shuddered and pictures fell off the wall. Even so, he insisted that not a blessed thing in this soulless place be changed. They had come to Chicago to dramatize the fact that for $90 per month slumlords gave poor blacks—who on the average earned $4,700 yearly—the opportunity to dwell, some families packed ten to a flat, in wretched dumps of such advanced rot and decay that each crumbling unpainted wall, each untiled floor, each broken-down radiator, each crisp roach egg in the cabinets, each dishrag curtain on the windows, and each rusted faucet reinforced the free-floating despair that if you lived here, where every particle of your physical surroundings induced shame and was one step up from trash, was a throwaway, was substandard, then the country must regard you as a throwaway too.

The hallway leading to his third-floor rooms was black-dark. The stairs trembled under his feet. He couldn't lock the front door, so winos were free to piss in the entryway. In other words, the place where he'd brought his family was a urinal. And he, even he, hated the climb up the rickety steps to the top of the stairs. High above his door a single tungsten bulb buzzed in a halo of swirling dust motes the last few seconds before its filament flimmered out. Inside, their four rooms—

hollow rinds filled with secondhand furniture—were arranged boxcar style (one for sitting, two for sleeping, and a miserable little kitchen) and were blisteringly hot and claustrophobic in the summer of 1966, even when his wife threw open the windows, for whatever breezes came through the rooms carried as well petroleum fumes and loud conversations and the roar of traffic from the streets below. Was this worth ninety dollars a month? Moreover, was proving his point by living here worth the toll he saw it taking on his family? The drain, the darkening of their spirits. "There's nothing green in sight," Coretta said, and for a moment he'd felt panicky, afraid, wondering if his work for his people, which he knew would kill him ("This is what is going to happen to me," he'd told her as they sat solemnly watching the news of John Kennedy's murder)—wondering if it would destroy his beautiful wife and four children as well.

In the last forty-eight hours, he'd survived a meeting with Richard Daley, from whom he'd won a few precious concessions (sprinklers attached to fire hydrants, swimming pools shipped to the West Side) that might defuse the potential for more rioting; then he'd gathered with gang members to sway them to the side of nonviolence, meetings so torn by conflict and shouting and hatred of the police that he had to make himself appear to be the person at fault in order to calm the others down. Having come through these crises, and with more to face, the man from whom the world expected everything, who sometimes went for days on four hours of sleep and rested fully only when he checked into a hospital, tried for a moment to nap, to step back from the severe discipline that black manhood called for in the twentieth century for just one precious moment in the sweltering heat of his Lawndale flat.

I

I knocked on his open bedroom door. "Doc?"

Rolling over, he crushed the lumpy pillow against his chest but kept his eyes closed, probably hoping whoever had come would go away, at least for a few moments more. Except for one other security person, we were alone in the apartment. His wife and children were staying at the home of Mahalia Jackson until the shooting died down. Later he would tell me he'd been dreaming of the sunset at Land's End, that breathtaking stretch of beach on Cape Comorin in the Hindu state of Kerala, which struck him as the closest thing to paradise when he and Coretta traveled to India: he dreamed an ancient village of brown-skinned people (Africa was in their ancestry) who knew their lord Vishnu by a thousand names, for He was imminent in the sky and sand, wood and stone, masquerading as Many. He'd come to India not as a celebrated civil rights leader but as a pilgrim. To learn. And though the promise of that pilgrimage was cut short when he plunged into the ongoing crisis back home, he had indeed learned much. Against the glorious sunset of Kerala, with the softest whisper of song carried on the wind from temples close by, *Ahimsa paramo dharma,* his wife took his hand and turned him to see the moon swell up from the sea, and in that evanescent instant, at the place where the Indian Ocean, the Arabian Sea, and the Bay of Bengal flowed together, he experienced an ineffable peace, and had never felt so free, and . . .

"Doc, I'm sorry to bother you," I said into the darkness. Though the lamps were off, burning fires outside the window pintoed his bedroom wall. "There's someone here to see you. I think you'd better take a look at him."

When he looked toward the door, toward me, I knew what he saw: a twenty-four-year-old with the large, penetrating "frog eyes" of his friend James Baldwin behind a pair of granny glasses, dehydrating and dripping sweat in brown trousers and a short-sleeved shirt weighted down by a battery of pencils and pens. I stepped into the room and walked directly to the window, looking down before I shut it on streets turned into combat zones as treacherous as any that year in Tay Ninh or Phnom Penh. The fuse: black kids cranking on fire hydrants. The flame: police trying to stop them. The consequence: a crowd that poured bricks and whiskey bottles and then ricocheting bullets from balconies and rooftops. It was not a night, July 17, to be out in bedlam unless you had to be. Firefighters dousing blazes set by roving street gangs had to be out there. Marksmen hunkered down behind their squad cars, praying that Governor Kerner would order, as promised, four thousand National Guardsmen into the city, had to be there—and so in a few short hours did the man whose sleep I had interrupted.

At the window, I could see two men shoot out the street-light at the intersection of Sixteenth Street and South Hamlin. Their first shots missed the target; then at last one struck, plunging the corner into darkness. A sound of shattering glass came from the grocery store on Sixteenth Street. The pistol fire had been so close, just below the window, it changed air pressure inside the building, tightening my inner ear. Roving gangs were setting cars on fire. Light from the interiors of torched cars threw shadows like strokes of tar across the bedroom's furnishings. Below the window figures darted furtively through the darkness, their colors and clans indistinguishable, slaying—or trying to slay—one another. I no longer knew on which side of this slaying I belonged. Or if there was any victory, pleasure, or Promised Land that could justify the killing and destruction of the past three nights.

I looked at the watch on my wrist. The luminous numerals read 8:15, but it felt more like midnight in the soul.

"Who is it?" The minister rubbed his eyes. "Is he here for the Agenda Committee meeting? Tell him I'll be ready in just a minute—"

"No, sir. He's outside in the hallway now. Reverend, I think you *need* to take a look at this."

After swinging his feet to the floor, he sat hunched forward, both elbows on his knees, waiting for his head to clear. I noticed he wore no cross around his neck. Nor did he need one. With his shirt open, there in the bedroom's heat, I could see the scar tissue shaped like a rood—a permanent one—over his heart, carved into his flesh by physician Aubre D. Maynard when he removed Izola Curry's letter opener from his chest in Harlem Hospital. I knew he was tired, and I did not rush him. His staff had been working off-the-clock since the West Side went ballistic. He hadn't slept in two days. Neither had I. All this night I'd drifted in and out of nausea, finding a clear space where I briefly felt fine, then as I heard the gunfire again, sirens, the sickness returned in spasms of dizziness, leaving me weak and overheated, then chilled.

He reached toward his nightstand for the wristwatch he'd left on top of a stack of books—*The Writings of Saint Paul*, Maritain's *Christianity and Democracy*, Nietzsche's *The Anti-Christ*—alongside the sermon he was preparing for the coming Sunday. Typically, his sermons took two-thirds of a day to compose. In them his conclusions were never merely closures but always seemed to be fresh starting points. The best were classically formal, intentionally Pauline, cautious at the beginning like the first hesitant steps up a steep flight of stairs, then each carefully chosen refrain pushed it higher, faster, with mounting intensity, toward a crescendo that fused antique form and African rhythms, Old Testament imagery and America's most cherished democratic ideals—principles dating back to the Magna Carta—into a shimmering creation, a synthesis so beautiful in the way his words alchemized the air in churches and cathedrals it could convert the wolf of Gubbio. He was, I realized again, a philosopher, which was something easy to forget (even for him) in a breathless year that began with the January murder of student Sammy Younge in Alabama, seventeen-year-old Jerome Huey beaten to death in Cicero in May, Fred Hubbard shot in April, Ben Chester White (Mississippi) and Clarence Triggs (Louisiana) killed by the Klan in June and July, the Georgia legislature's refusal to seat Julian Bond in February because of his opposition to the Vietnam War, Kwame Nkrumah deposed as Ghana's leader the same month, then the slaughter of eight Chicago student nurses by a madman named Richard Speck. Not until I saw the books by his bed did I recall that in a less tumultuous time he taught Greek thought to a class of Morehouse students, among them

Julian Bond, who testified that King, a freshly minted Ph.D., often looked up from his notes, closed his copy of Plato's collected dialogues, and brought whole cloth out of his head passages from Socrates' apology, emphasizing the seventy-one-year-old sage's reply to his executioners, "I would never submit wrongly to any authority through fear of death, but would refuse even at the cost of my life."

After turning his watch-stem a few times, he squinted up at me, searching his mind for my name. I could tell he remembered me only as one of his organization's many, nameless volunteers.

"I know I've seen you, um—"

"Matthew, sir. Matthew Bishop."

"Oh yes, of course," he said.

Although he took great care to put everyone on his staff at ease, I'd always felt awkward and off-balance on the few occasions I'd been in his presence; I'd never seemed able to say the right things or find a way to stand or sit that didn't betray how disbelieving I was that he was talking to someone who had as little consequence in this world (or the next) as I did. As he pulled on his shoes, I guessed straightaway what he was thinking: I was not making sense, nor was I much to look at. I knew I left no lasting impression on people who met me once (and often two and three times). Most never remembered my name. I had no outstanding features, no "best side," as they say, to hold in profile. During SCLC meetings, a demonstration, rally, or march, I blended easily into the background, as bland and undistinguished as a piece of furniture, so anonymous most people forgot I was there. I was no taller than the minister himself, but much thinner: a shy, bookish man who went to great lengths not to call unnecessary attention to himself. I kept my hair neatly trimmed, wore respectable shoes, and always had a book or magazine nearby to flip open when I found myself alone,

25

which, as it turned out, was most of the time, even when I was in a crowd. I was nobody. A man reminded of his mediocrity—and perishability—nearly every moment of the day. A nothing. Merely a face in the undifferentiated mass of Movement people who dutifully did what our leaders asked, feeling sometimes like a cog in a vast machine—I did feel that way often: replaceable like the placards we made for a march, or the flyers we plastered all over the city, only to paper over them with new pages a week later.

Then why did I join? My mother revered Dr. King. And I did too. Compared with the minister and his family, who were Georgia brahmins, the closest thing black America had to a First Family, we were at best among the "little people," like the inconspicuous disciple Andrew, destined to run their errands and man their ditto machines on the margins of history. Nevertheless, my mother (to me) was regal, aristocratic by virtue of her actions: a sister to Mother Pollard who, when stopped by reporters during the Montgomery boycott, said, "My feets is tired but my soul is rested." It was that woman and my mother King had in mind when in his 1955 speech at the Holt Street Baptist Church he said, "When the history books are written in future generations, the historians will have to pause and say, 'There lived a great people—a black people—who injected new meaning into the veins of civilization.'" That was true of him, of course. History knew nothing of Ellesteen Bishop. Since her death it was as if she'd never lived, and now only existed in memory, in me during those times when I thought of her, which were less and less each year, and when I ceased to be, it seemed to me, all vestiges of her would vanish as well. (Often I tried to reconstruct her face, and found I could not remember, say, her ears. How could I forget my own mother's ears?) In her mind, the minister was a saint. She'd kept his portrait right beside photos of Jesus and John Fitzgerald Kennedy over her bed. More than anything I wanted to help the Movement that had meant so much to her, to do something for *him*, since I was, as I said, a man of no consequence at all.

"It's good to see young people like yourself helping out," the minister said. "How old did you say you were?"

"Twenty-four."

"Relax, there's no need to be nervous. Tell me, what exactly do you *do* around here?"

"Whatever needs doing. Sometimes it's filing," I said. "Other times it's taking notes at meetings and getting out flyers. For the last week I've been chauffeuring your wife to speeches on the North Side and sticking around evenings to help Amy watch the apartment. It gives me a chance to catch up on my studies."

"You're in school, then?"

"I was . . . until last year. I left when my mother passed."

"I'm sorry," he said, nodding. "And your father—"

"I never knew him."

He glanced away, clearing his throat. "What were you working on? In school, I mean."

"Philosophy."

All at once his eyes brightened, as if I'd called the name of an old friend. "When there's time," he said, "you should let me look over some of your papers. It's been a while since I've had a chance to put everything aside and freely discuss ideas. Who were you reading?"

"I left off with Nietzsche."

From the distaste on his face, the deep frown, one would have thought I'd said I was studying the Devil.

"Have you read Brightman?"

"Not yet."

"Do," he urged. "No one else makes perfect sense to me. Get the Nietzsche out of your system. He's seductive for children—all that lust for power—but he's really the one we're fighting against." He stood up, reaching into his wrinkled suitcoat slung over the back of a bedside chair for a pack of cigarettes. "Think about it."

"I will, sir, except right now we've got something . . . pretty strange outside."

"Strange?" He pursed his lips. "You didn't say anything about strange before. Let me have it."

"I think you need to see him for yourself."

Wearily, he pulled on his wrinkled suitcoat, then his shoes. I could see that the short nap had helped not at all. The grumbling of his belly told me he must be hungry, that he hadn't eaten a decent meal in a day and a half, but checking the flat's refrigerator, which never kept anything cold, would have to wait until he faced the unsettling reason I'd disturbed his slumber. Another leader, I knew, might have sent me away, calling attention to his trials, his suffering, his fatigue. For King that was out of character. Too many times he'd said, "It is possible for one to be self-centered in his self-sacrifice"—in other words, to use the pain of performing the Lord's work to seek pity and sympathy. No, he never dwelled upon himself, and, although tired, he buttoned his suitcoat and stepped with jelly-legged exhaustion from the darkened bedroom, forcing his lips into a smile as he followed me down the hallway to the living room.

Waiting in the kiln-hot kitchen, seated in a straight-backed chair, was Amy. I felt her presence before my eyes found the imprint of the simple cross under her white blouse, her denim skirt, and the Afro, an aureole black as crow's feathers, framing her face. She kept pushing a pair of black, owl-frame glasses back up the narrow bridge of her nose—a student's gesture, I'd thought during the first few weeks when she volunteered for the Coordinating Council of Community Organizations. Her voice was low and smoky.

Some nights it ran rill-like through my head. She was a Baptist, raised since the age of six by her grandmother on Chicago's South Side after the death of her mother following a beating—one of many—from her father, who worked for the railroad and gambled away his meager earnings at the race track. Thus it was her grandmother—Mama Pearl, as she called her—who'd taken care of Amy. Earlier that summer she'd invited Mama Pearl to drop by the Lawndale flat and meet the minister. And so she did, wheezing up the stairs, crepitations like crackling cellophane sounding in her chest with each breath, struggling with her body's adipose freight, hauling a brown weathered handbag big enough for a child to crawl into, and announced, "Usually I don't go nowhere on the third. That's when my husband comes." For a second she watched King mischievously, then said, "You don't know what I'm talking about, do you?"

He shook his head.

"I calls my disability check my husband, it comes on the third," and she cackled wildly. The staff fell in love with her that day, with her feathery wig that knocked twenty years off her total of seventy-eight, with the way she worked her toothless mouth like a fish while listening to King explain his plans in Chicago, bobbing her head and asking, "Is you, really?" with her head pushed forward, wig askew, and feet planted apart in two shapeless black shoes. She was utterly unselfconscious. Egoless, and flitted round the flat as though she had feet spun from air. Descending like twin trees from her checkered dress were two vein-cabled legs, lumpy in places, bowed, but it was her voice that everyone remembered most. Thinking she might be thirsty, I offered her a soda, which she declined, shaking her head and explaining, "Thank you, dah'ling, I'm tickled, but I bet' not drink no pop, I might pee on myself." Her bag was filled with medicine for her heart and high blood pressure, ills of which she was heedless, saying, "Naw, I ain't supposed to eat salt, but I eats it anyway. I eats *any*thing."

In point of fact, Mama Pearl was everybody's grandmother. "There wasn't nothin' I didn't do in the fields," she said, speaking of her childhood in southern Illinois. Now she lived on Stony Island in a seventy-five-dollar-a-month walkup with no running water, where she passed her time crocheting (she gave the minister a quilt she'd worked on for two years), "eye-shopping" (as she put it) in downtown stores, and fishing, which was her passion. She'd go with what she called another "senior" or Amy, having her granddaughter lug along a bulging bag of fried chicken, cookies, grapes and peaches, a few ribs, and a thermos. For Mama Pearl fishing was a social event, one to be shared as you ate and talked and played whist. Standing ankle-deep in the water, she'd throw out her line, but was almost too afraid of saltwater worms to slice and bait them (they were hairy and huge and had serrated teeth like a saw). During her afternoon at the flat, she brought forth from her enormous bag three canisters of her own home-cooked raspberry, apricot, and cinnamon rugelach, which she distributed to the entire staff. She inspected everything, involved herself with everyone, including me ("Now, you don't mind my bein' nosy, do you, Matthew? I was jes ovah there talkin' to that light-skinned fellah and he didn't mind"), and giggled like a young girl, "Ain't I somethin'?" Before leaving she collected SCLC stationery as souvenirs for the other "seniors" in her church and, waving good-bye at the door, assured us all that "I had a re-e-e-al fine time."

So had we all, especially King, who kissed her hand as she left (again she giggled), and Amy, who seemed aglow whenever she looked at the grandmother who'd taught her Scripture and how to be a woman, how to crochet, that she could use a string and old tin can for fishing just as easily as a pole and line, and that at all times she must remember others. Yes, she'd taken care of Amy well, raising her—or so I thought—to be as pure in love and self-forgetfulness and service as herself, though Amy at twenty, with her brilliant Dorothy Dandridge smile, was drop-dead beautiful. She did not eat meat. Synthetic fabrics, she said, gave her a rash. She had briefly studied drama and modern dance at Columbia College, where I'd first seen her in the hallways, but then she ran short on funds and took whatever temporary job turned up—short-order cook, dayworker, then watching the Lawndale flat after I'd recommended her for the job.

I had my reasons for that.

Compared with her, I was shy and unsure of myself in everything except my studies. Most of the time feelings banged and knocked through me like something trying to break free from inside. But I screwed up my courage and asked her out to dinner a week after she came to work. Amy thought about my request for a moment, her head cocked to one side, and simply replied, "I don't eat." I never had the courage to ask her again.

To avoid her eyes, I turned to the minister, who said, "Well, where is he?"

"I told him to wait outside on the steps," Amy said, pulling her skirt down a little. "I'll get him. You two go on back to the kitchen. Matthew, show him the I.D."

The minister asked, "What I.D.?"

From my shirt pocket I extracted a dog-eared card. "She means this."

The card I handed over as we walked back down the hallway was an expired Illinois state driver's license issued to one Chaym Smith, birth date 01/15/29, height 5'7", weight 180, eyes brown. The minister gazed—and gazed—at the worn license, picking at his lip, and finally looked back at me, poking the card with his finger.

"This could be *me*!"

"That's what we thought too," I said.

"Who is this man?"

"We don't know."

"But what does he want with me?"

"Sir," I said, "maybe he should tell you himself."

I could see the minister was impatient now for some explanation. Minutes passed. In the kitchen, the wall clock ticked softly beside an *Ebony* magazine calendar. Food smells, sour and sharp, floated from the sink and an unemptied, paper-lined garbage pail beside it. Then from the front room we could hear the door open. Outside, sirens pierced the hot night air. The neighborhood dogs howled. Through the window, I saw flames from burning cars dancing against a dark sky skirling with tear gas and smoke. The night felt wrong. All of it, as if the riot, the looting and lunacy, breakdown and disorder, had torn space and time, destroying some delicate balance or barrier between dimensions—possible worlds—creating a portal for fantastic creatures to pour through. I could not shake that feeling, and it grew all the stronger when Amy entered the kitchen with the man whose driver's license I'd handed to King. A man without father or mother, like the priest Melchizedek who mysteriously appeared in the Valley of Siddim after the king of Sodom rebelled against Chedorlaomer.

Stepping back a foot, King whispered, "Sweet Jesus . . ."

"I thought you'd be interested," I said.

Far beyond interested, he looked spellbound. Then shaken. He might have been peering into a mirror, one in which his history was turned upside down, beginning not in his father's commodious, two-story Queen Anne–style home in Atlanta but instead across the street in one of the wretched shotgun shacks crammed with the black poor. Certainly in every darkened, musty pool hall, on every street corner, in every cramped prison cell he'd passed through, the minister had seen men like Chaym Smith—but never quite like this.

He tore his eyes away, then looked back. Smith was still there, his eyes squinted, the faint smile on his lips one part self-protective irony, two parts sarcasm, as if he carried unsayable secrets (or sins) that, if spoken, would send others running from the room. His workshirt was torn in at least two places, and yellowed by his life in it; his trousers were splotchy with undecipherable stains and threadbare at the knees—he was the kind of Negro the Movement had for years kept away from the world's cameras: sullen, ill-kept, the very embodiment of the blues. Then, as the minister knuckled his eyes, Smith, behind his heavy black eyeglasses, beneath his bushy, matted hair and scraggly beard—as rubicund in tint as Malcolm Little's—began to look less threatening and more like a poor man down on his luck for a long, long time, one who'd probably not eaten in a week. Neglected like the very building we were in. Everything about him was in disrepair. Just as the city's administration and the flat's landlord, a white man named John Bender (who was hardly better off than his tenants), had failed to invest in the crumbling eyesore and allowed it to degenerate into a dilapidated, dangerous public health hazard, so no one, it seemed, had invested in Chaym Smith.

For a moment, the minister looked faint. His right hand reached for the back of a kitchen chair to anchor the spinning room and steady himself. He took a deep breath, then shook his visitor's hand and motioned for him to sit down at the table. "When they said I needed to *see* you, I had no idea—"

Smith's lips lifted ever so slightly at the corners. "Thank you for taking the time to see somebody like me, Reverend. I know you busy. But, I swear, ever since nineteen fifty-four, people been telling me I got a twin. Looks is about all we got in common, though. People love you. Especially white people. Sometimes"—he laughed again, at himself it seemed— "I figured God fucked up and missed with me, but He had you for backup." Smith peered down at his hands, squeezing them together. A dollop of sweat slid from his hairline down his cheek to his chin, and suddenly I had the feeling he was acting, playing a role he'd rehearsed many times, even using black English—a pâté of urban slang and southern idioms— playfully, as one would a toy. "I've read your books. Everything I could about you. Caught you on TV more times than I can count. So when I heard you were in Chicago, I figured I had to come by and at least shake your hand."

"You live here, then?" asked King.

"All my life, mainly on the South Side. That's where I grew up, in one of the county's juvenile homes. I reckon I been everywhere and done a li'l bit of everything. Most of it"—he laughed again—"come to a whole lot of nothing. Not like with you. I went in the service when I was twenty, the year after Truman signed Executive Order 9981. That put me right in the middle of Korea, but I was lucky, you know? I cruised through two years without a scratch. Guess it was 'cause I was on my knees every night, praying God'd get me outta there safely. See, I trusted Him. That's how I was raised. 'Bout a month before I was to fly home, I was filling out college entrance forms. Day before my plane left, I walked outside the base to celebrate with a buddy of mine named Stackhouse and smoke a li'l Korean boo—and what you think! My boot-heel came right down on a land mine. I left part of my leg—and all of Stackhouse—back in Pyongyang."

Smith lifted his left trouser leg, and my stomach lurched. The sweep of his shin was crooked. Brown flesh below the knob of his knee was twisted, muscleless, blackened as crisp

34

and crinkly as cellophane. Amy's hands flew to her lips, stifling a moan. And then, suddenly, Smith looked straight at me, flashing that ironical, almost erotic smirk again, as if somehow we were co-conspirators, or maybe he knew something scandalous about me, though we'd met only minutes earlier.

"The doctors spent a year rebuilding that from the femur to the metatarsal. My jaws were wired for months. Reverend, I tell you, after that—after my discharge—I just drifted and drank. I stayed in the East, sorta like being in exile, till I healed. I knew every bartender by his first name in Kyoto, Jakarta, and Rangoon. Finally come back to the States, and got me a li'l room at 3721 Indiana Avenue, and I was doin' okay for a while, trying to stay dry and go to school over at Moody Bible Institute—I always wanted to preach—then things kinda . . . fell apart for me again . . ."

The minister bent forward, squeezing his hands, unaware he was mirroring perfectly Smith's posture. "How do you mean?"

Smith drew a deep breath. (King took one too, as if slowly they were slipping into synchronization.) "I ain't sure what happened. I don't look for trouble, sir, but sometimes trouble just comes looking for me. Maybe it's bad karma, or something's wrong with my *ch'i* like they say in the East, I can't figure it."

He was working nights as a custodian, said Chaym Smith, and taking classes in the day. Back then he was an insatiable reader, the sort of autodidact who (like Harlem Renaissance writer Wallace Thurman) could absorb whole paragraphs at a single glance; his recall was so good he barely had to study for his exams. Sometimes when he came home three young boys—Powell, Jay, and Lester—would be playing on the steps or directly in front of the building in the street. They were good kids, he thought. Wild, but that was because each of them had a different father. In effect, no father. And with no Daddy, they saw everything—and any-thing—as permissible. He knew what that was, not knowing your father, but feeling that the indifferent sonuvabitch who brought you into the world was out there somewhere, face-less and unreachable, silent and remote, someone you needed and hated all at the same time until the moment came that you damned him, renounced Him, and moved on. Nearly every day Smith saw those boys, and he liked them—he bought the trio candy and *Tales of the Unexpected* comic books at the corner store, shot a few hoops with them on Saturday when he was tired of studying, and after getting permission from their mother, Juanita Lomax, who was young and pretty and seemed to like him whenever she bumped into Smith in the hallway, he drove them in his bat-tered secondhand Corvair to see Sidney Poitier's portrayal of a black soldier in Korea in *All the Young Men*. It reminded him of his time in Korea, and he hoped Juanita's boys would pick up something positive from Poitier's performance, though he couldn't be sure they had, given the way Powell and Jay hooted and threw popcorn at the screen when Alan Ladd's bigoted character came on. Still, they told him they'd had a great evening when Smith brought them back to their mother's basement apartment.

As it turned out, Juanita was not there when he brought her boys home. Thing is, this was nothing new. Often she left them alone to fend for and feed themselves, usually potatoes, which they peeled with a pocketknife, threw into a handleless skillet in the closet-sized kitchen, then proceeded to burn until the four dark, below-ground rooms, which always smelled damp, clouded with smoke. Smith always worried they'd set the place on fire. That night, however, he'd filled their stomachs at White Castle, so he was sure they'd do no cooking and go straight to bed.

His own tiny but tidy room was three flights up, one of the front bedrooms in a flat rented by Vera Thomas—a kind, brown-skinned woman about thirty—and her mother, an elderly woman who often said she wished he, Smith, had been her son, what with the way he studied and worked so hard after he got out of the service, and him with a disability too. Smith said he turned his key in the door and walked through the darkened living room—it was by then nearly midnight—then entered his bedroom, clicking on the light. Under his covers, wearing only a smile, was Juanita. Vera, she said, let her into his room when she explained he was out with her boys. She had something to give him to express her thanks for his being so kind to her kids. He asked her what that was. She said, Come here and see. Although he could not remember undressing, or the details of what he said—or might have promised her—Smith spent that night under the covers with Juanita Lomax.

The next week he was in court.

How he got there even he couldn't rightly say. The police had picked him up on his job. Later he learned that Juanita had sworn on a stack of Bibles that he'd forced himself on her. Fortunately for Smith, this was not a case the judge wanted to hear. Juanita argued—as she had twice earlier in the same court—that he was obliged to make her an honorable woman. No, the judge said, he would have to do nothing of the kind. He lectured Juanita not to take up the court's time this way again, but once they were outside again on the street, her waiting at the bus stop and crying, he stepped up behind her and said yes, he would marry her, if that was what she wanted.

King lit a fresh cigarette off the one he had going. "Was that what *you* wanted?"

Smith shrugged. "I guess so. I wanted them boys to have a father. I figured Juanita'n me could come together on that."

"I think you did an honorable thing."

"Naw." Again, that satiric grin. "I was a fool."

He'd tried, said Smith, to provide for the boys and their mother, but maybe—who knows?—he didn't try hard enough or just wasn't meant to be married, or maybe he had an inverted Midas touch so that everything he brushed against transmogrified into crap. He gave up going to school, he got a second job with a moving company, and after two years he was able to get them into a bigger place, a housing project, in Altgeld Gardens, though it seemed like even with two jobs there was hardly anything left at the end of the month after he paid the bills, and somehow—he wasn't sure how—what little was left he wound up putting on another bottle of whiskey because he needed that to wind down and get to sleep some nights; and there wasn't much time either to go to church after he took a third job as a night watchman on the weekends, or to spend with the boys, who started cutting school and keeping bad company, or with Juanita, who, he discovered, liked Colombian Gold as much as he did Johnny Walker (Black), so much so—according to one of his neighbors—that she slipped away in the afternoons when he was working to see another man who sold exactly what she wanted, though his neighbor said *he* had no idea how Juanita was paying for it, and when he confronted her with this the fights began, him accusing her of infidelity, her damning him for his drinking, their shouting going on sometimes all night, so loud other residents threatened to call the police, and her boys couldn't bear that, naturally; they took to staying away from the place as long as they could, and after a time so did he, feeling thankful he was so mired in nickel-dime jobs that he had a way to escape that household, escape thinking about himself, escape the near hysteria he felt when he realized his life was a nightmare, a ghastly joke on everything he'd once dreamed of becoming. He rode the streets for hours some evenings after work, simply to avoid returning home, and it was on one such night in 1963, after cruising the South Side until he was nearly out of gas, that he realized he didn't have the faintest idea where the hell he lived. Try as he might, he could not remember the address or recognize the street. Other things were gone too, whole quadrants of his memory. Unable to get home, he pulled up in front of a police station and told them his predicament, and they held him overnight for evaluation.

They held him for a long time, first at the station, then at an institution in Elgin, because when the police knocked on his door, discovered it open, then stepped inside, they found Juanita's three boys strangled in their beds and pieces of their mother distributed here and there throughout the apartment. When they told him, Smith wept in his cell. He swore he knew nothing about it. Twice he passed a polygraph test. They could not convict him of the crime, but they did send him to Elgin, where he worked sometimes in the kitchen, sometimes with other patients cleaning up the grounds around the hospital, and met with doctors who spent two years helping him patch together the broken pieces of his personality. When he was released, there was nowhere for him to go except to Vera Thomas, who gave him back his old room and accepted the little he could offer her from what he made doing odd jobs, here and there, on the South Side.

After a silence, Smith and King drew breath at the same instant. The minister let Smith speak first.

"Like I said, Reverend, I been tryin' like hell to get back on my feet, to do somethin' worthwhile with my life."

"If we can achieve our goals for equality here, I think things will be better for you."

"What if you don't?"

"Excuse me?" The minister scratched his cheek.

"I guess you think the Lord puts us all here with a definite purpose, don't you?"

"That's right. Everyone is equal in His eyes."

"I don't see that."

King was silent, perhaps uncertain of what to say, or so challenged by the sharpness of Smith's voice that his own thoughts were stilled.

"Sir, I *need* work. That's all I'm asking for. Right now I can't rub two dimes together. Problem is, there ain't too many places that'll hire me. But I figure there *is* maybe one thing I *can* do, if you're willin', and I been praying night and day you will be."

"What is that?"

"I read that when you was in Montgomery you got over forty death threats a day—is that so?"

"Yes," the minister said, nodding, "and I still get them."

"That woman who stabbed you? Weren't you signing books when that happened? The knife come within an inch of your heart, didn't it?"

"Yes."

"I coulda been there instead of you," said Smith.

"What?"

"When you go somewhere or leave a place, I could be there too, and if somebody's tryin' to hurt you, they won't know whichaway to turn. That's all I'm askin', that you let me do somethin'—maybe the only thing in this world—I *can* do."

"No." The minister stood up so suddenly the back of his legs sent his chair skidding a foot behind him. "Absolutely not. I could never agree to anything like that."

Smith smiled bitterly. "Thought you might say that. You ain't the first person to turn me away. Or to take a shot at me 'cause I favor you so much."

"What did you say?"

"I said I been catching hell since you come to Chicago.

Last week a couple of boys pushed me off the El platform."
Smith measured five inches between his forefinger and
thumb. "I was 'bout *that* far from landin' on the third rail.
Lots of people know where you're stayin' in town, but some
don't. They see me and come to *my* place. Some of 'em tore
up my room. Scared my landlady so much she's askin' me to
leave. But where am I gonna go? Hell, I can't walk down the
street or go to the store without somebody stoppin' me.
Some of 'em spit in my face. That's colored as well as white.
That's why I come here. I figure if I'm catchin' hell 'cause of
you, I might's well catch it *for* you instead."

"You've no place to stay?"

"Not after tomorrow."

The minister made a sharp intake of breath. He rubbed
the back of his neck, then paced back and forth in the
kitchen, perhaps thinking—as I had been all evening—of
that ancient Christian story of the couple who found a
bedraggled old man at their door, invited him inside, fed and
comforted him, and only after their guest left discovered he
was the Nazarene. Finally King took his seat. "Would you all
come here with me at the table? Mr. Smith has suffered
much. I'd like to say a prayer for him."

Amy and I sat down; she was to my left, the minister to
my right, and Smith directly in front of me. We joined hands
and closed our eyes. Looking back, I cannot recall the whole
content of King's prayer, but it was appropriate, an affirma-
tion that all, regardless of circumstance, were loved by the
Lord. And I would not have opened my eyes before he'd finished, but I felt pressure beneath the table on my left foot, a
gentle tapping like a lover's signal. Thinking this was Amy,
hoping it was so, I let my lids blink open, and saw that Smith
had never closed his eyes. He was staring at us—like a fugi-
tive peering at a comfortable bourgeois family through their
window as they eat dinner, oblivious to his presence—and on

his face was that unsettling smile as he critically scrutinized King, then Amy, who gripped his hand tightly (heaven knows what she was thinking). And then, tilting his head, tapping my foot again, he winked.

I felt my face stretch. I squeezed shut my eyes, but his afterimage burned in the space behind my lids long after the prayer was done.

King turned to Smith and said, "Could you step outside?"

After Smith left, the minister rubbed his forehead. "I swear to God, I don't know how to help this man, but I feel we should do something for him. What he proposes . . . it's just too dangerous!"

"Sir," I said, "it sounds like he's already a target. You might say his resemblance to you has marked him."

"Yes, yes." He kneaded his lower lip. "Amy, when your grandmother was here, did Mama Pearl say she grew up downstate?"

"Yes," said Amy. "Her old house is there. It's empty. No one is living there now."

"Could he stay there?"

"I guess so."

"I'd like you and Matthew to stay with him, at least until the disturbance is over and we're finished here in Chicago. I want you to work with him. Get him back on his feet. Help him understand what the Movement's about—and have him sign the Commitment Blank."

"What about you?" Amy asked. "Won't you need us here?"

"I think we'll be all right. We'll find somebody to replace you." He stepped toward the kitchen door. Turning, he added, "I'll see that you're both compensated for this, of course," and then he started toward the bedroom and stopped. "One other thing."

"Yes, sir?"

"You keep that man away from my wife, you hear?"

I assured him we would not let Smith, who was still waiting outside, anywhere near his family. I walked down the hallway, opened the front door, and found our visitor sitting on the top step, smoking. Keeping a few feet between us, I said, "Chaym, it's okay. Doc's going to find something for you to do." Cautiously, I smiled. "He thinks you might be able to help."

"Yeah, and maybe I can do something special for you too. You interest me, Bishop. You've got promise."

"For what?"

The only answer Smith gave was his mocking, mordant grin.

I swallowed with difficulty. When I spoke, my voice splintered, and he seemed to enjoy that. "I'll call you tomorrow with more details. Is that all right? I really do hope he gives you a job."

"A job?" Now Smith was descending the first few steps into the shadows, his profile lighted in such a way that I could see only fragments of his face, like pieces of an unfinished puzzle, or a mask. "I don't want just a job, Bishop. Uh-uh. I want a li'l of what the good doctor in there has got in such great abundance."

"What is that?"

Now I could see his face not at all, though I heard his shoes striking the lower stair treads, and from below, on the lightless levels where he stood, like a voice rising up beneath the ground, I thought I heard him say, *Immortality.*

2

Hours after his visitor left, he tried again to rest, knowing he should, not for himself but for the others who depended upon him being at his best. Lying awake, tossing and turning, he looked back on his life and saw only a gauntlet of work, ever more difficult exercises in giving. In the corner a dented fan clacked as its blades turned. He'd kicked his bedcovers onto the floor and sprawled on his back in teal-blue pajamas with gold piping on the placket and around the neck, hoping if he was motionless sleep might come. But his mind churned on. He squinted at the ceiling where he saw, in broken plaster, the face of the strange man who had shaken his certainty that all were equal in the eyes of the Lord. The words still echoed in the deepest coils of his ears. Words Smith had almost hissed, hurling them at him like stones and with such hurt that he, about to open his mouth in a parable, offering one of his stan-

dard apothegms for suffering, stopped as if he'd been slapped. All his explanations were suspended, bracketed, and shimmering in their place was the ineluctable presence of this man who could have been his brother were it not for the fact that he appeared to be damned. Or fallen.

Yes, he could admit it now: their physical likeness frightened him. What were the chances of encountering a double for oneself? Yet there he'd been, as if his own father had spit them out one, two. Like that. And what had he wanted? A job as his decoy? My God, didn't he have enough trouble already? How strange it always was: someone standing before him, wanting something, and even more incredible than their desire was the belief that he could actually do something for them. (Things had reached a point where he even had to be careful how he complimented others in his letters because some would excerpt his praise, without his permission, in letters of reference.) In the apartment's close air, in the narrow hallway, in the kitchen, Smith's scent and vestigial spirit lingered, as if he'd subtly altered the flat—nothing felt the same after his appearance. He'd retreated to the bedroom after the man left.

But it was not this feeling of displacement that now kept him awake, endlessly readjusting the lumpy pillow beneath his head. It was what Smith had said. The acuity, the clarity with which he'd dismissed "equality" and all that hallowed word implied. There in the predawn shadows, in the unveiling parenthesis into which Smith's coming placed his most cherished beliefs, he wondered if perhaps it was no more than a word, an abstraction, empty sound signifying nothing. A chimera at the Movement's core, in fact, the very centerpiece of Jefferson's magnificent declaration, We hold these truths to be self-evident, that all men are created equal. Across America, from one platform and podium to the next, he'd sung that sacred principle—equality—as his strongest, last best hope for

*proclaiming that Americans could not live up to their bedrock
ideals if Negroes were disenfranchised. Even his critics tipped
lightly around this metaphysical trump card. Still, a few tried,
albeit timidly (so as not to seem like bigots), the casuists eager
to point out that no two things in Nature were equal. Believing so, they said, was simply formulating sincerity (and senti-
mentality) into dogma. All right, he'd replied. Fine. On the
face of things, Nature was unjust. Who could deny that? But
in the realm of the spirit invoked by the Founders, in God,
there were no defensible social distinctions, for all creatures
great and small, black and white, were isomers of the divine
Person. It was a shamelessly Platonic argument, he knew that,
yet of its veracity he'd been so sure.*

At least until now.

*He rolled to the side of the bed, the springs in his mattress
squeaking; his fingers fumbled on the nightstand, then found
his watch and cigarettes. The glowing, beryline numbers read
4:30. In an hour it would be daybreak. He knew that as soon
as sunlight knifed through the windows he wouldn't sleep.
After taking off his pajama top, moist and clammy and cling-
ing to his body, he padded barefoot and barechested along the
buckled, pewter-gray linoleum to the bathroom, sweat like a
sprinkling of silver along his shoulders and chest. When he
pulled the light bulb's chain, a cataract of black and brown
cockroaches in the porcelain sink, on the walls, and in the
tiny claw-footed bathtub scrambled away from the light. They
fled behind the cabinet and into the cracks where floor and
walls joined, some dragging translucent lunular eggs behind
them. Instantly he felt ill. Since he'd moved into the flat they
were in his food, his clothing, his luggage. One had crawled
out of his suitcoat when he was in a meeting, dropping
obscenely onto the papers spread before him at the conference
table. Filthy things! he thought. A constant companion of the
poor. When he was eight, his mother told him that where you*

46

saw one, you could bet there were hundreds more hidden. All at once he was tempted to quash them into pulp with his fingers. But no. He pulled back, willing himself away from violence, remembering the holy men he'd seen one night in Kerala, the twig-broom-carrying Jain priests who killed nothing, ever, and swept in front of themselves as they walked so as not to harm creatures too small to see. They walked in these words: Whatever it is, it is you. No, as much as he might want to, he could not harm even these loathsome things without harming himself. The exercise of reining in his revulsion would do him good, he thought, maybe even make him thankful to something he hated for giving him the opportunity to work through his disgust. So he waited, taking long breaths to steady himself, watching them flee and wondering, until the last one disappeared, if Chaym awoke every day to a crawling bathroom like this.

He ran warm water (it seldom got cold) into his cupped hands, splashed it onto his face, and, looking up, peered at himself in the tiny cabinet mirror above the sink, experimentally touching his cheeks, his chin (he realized he needed to shave), and tracing two fingers across the length of his mustache. My face, he thought. And Chaym's. But in no other way than the somatic were they equal. In fact, they were like negatives of each other. He laughed, humorlessly. The idea of justice in his life and Chaym's was a joke. Not only was the distribution of wealth in society grossly uneven, he thought, but so was God-given talent. Beauty. Imagination. Luck. And the blessing of loving parents. They were the products of the arbitrariness of fortune. You could not say they were deserved.

He stared at his (their) image in the mirror, remembering simultaneously with pride and pain, gratitude and guilt, that of everyone in his family he himself had easily the greatest oratorical skills. They outstripped those of his own father, his grandfather, and, to be honest, everyone else he knew. Some *resented him for that. Down deep, he could not deny that his dearest friend, Ralph Abernathy, loved and bitterly envied the range and reach of erudition in his sermons. He did not want to recall how many times he'd poured himself, heart and soul, into his preaching only to have another, older minister with a room-temperature I.Q. clap him on the back when he was done, and say, with a smile that never reached his eyes, "Man, I hate you." Or the jealous ones, no deeper than a dime, who talked about him behind his back as if he had a tail, and cornered him after his roof-raising sermons, and whispered this knife between his ribs, "No wonder them white folks want to integrate with you." He'd never known exactly how to respond to their envy. He knew—and they knew—that although his gifts were a devastating weapon against racism, they separated him from them. The irony of his situation never escaped him: excellence brought praise—so often from whites—but also the danger of his becoming a pariah among Negroes if he didn't somehow soften the separateness, the chasm his talent created between himself and others. Most of the time he played by those cutting remarks, or said something self-effacing, or quoted Jesus in Matthew 19:17* (Why callest thou me good? There is none good but . . . God), *or he simply tried to do more for the bruised ministers who felt threatened by him, lavishly praising them to their congregations. In a democracy where all were purportedly equal, it was so important to do that, assuage the egos of those he'd left behind. What else could he do? At Morehouse he'd considered other careers—the law, medicine—until his junior year, when the Lord let him see how the Negro church, despite its emotionalism, might become a vehicle for the most sophisticated modern thinking. This, he realized, he could do. He could not sing like Belafonte, portray a character like Robeson, punch like Joe Louis, write a poem like Claude McKay, draw bitingly satiric cartoons like Ollie Harrington, or paint colorful, delicately bal-*

anced canvases like Jacob Lawrence. He was called to preach. It was his talent, but oh my, what of those who had no talent to speak of?

He pulled a comb through his hair, brushed his teeth, clicked off the bathroom light, and stepped into the kitchen, where, as soon as he entered, he found Smith's odor—a commingling of tobacco and creosote—drifting sharply on the air. Coughing, he went back to the bedroom, carried his fan into the kitchen, and plugged it in on the counter. Then he opened the refrigerator, found a plate of Mama Pearl's delicious apricot rugelach wrapped in foil and a half-finished can of Coca-Cola, and took these back to the table, where he nibbled and let his thoughts go where they would. To his first meeting of the day, with the Agenda Committee. To Chaym. And then to the more troubling stories in the Book. One especially bothered him. The tale of two brothers. One's offering God accepted, the other He rejected. Was not the one spurned, who brought murder into the world—by killing the source of that inequality—the first revolutionary to defy favoritism and an unjust authority? He let this unwanted idea unwind, moving him farther back to the revolt of angels led by one of ensorcelling beauty who would not acquiesce to servitude and an inferior status, for even in heaven there was a caste system. Seraphim, it was said, loved deepest; cherubim knew the most.

He pushed away his plate and rubbed his eyes, unwilling to think longer along these lines. A soft belch lifted from his belly, barely audible above the smear of noises from the street below—traffic, the hissing tires of a bus passing by. The kitchen clock read 5:30. Sunlight yeasted in the kitchen, slowly brightening the room and his spirits as well. He lit a cigarette and thought: yes, inequality was stitched into the fabric of Being. No one deserved greater natural gifts than others. But despite the fortuitous differences in men, they could volunteer to share one another's fate. They could—in fact, should—rearrange the social world to redress the arbitrary whims of contingency, accident, and chance. If the fortunate did not help, rancor and bloodshed might never cease. The least advantaged had every right to break the social contract that had so miserably failed to meet their needs. They would rebel, riot as they were doing now in Chicago. For their own sake and survival, God's favored had to lift those on whom He'd turned His back.

Morning pushed aside the previous night's shadows. He stubbed out his cigarette in a bean-bag ashtray, considered again the case of Chaym Smith, then dug a finger into his mouth to dislodge a sliver of rugelach stuck in his dental work, feeling at last comfortable with this decision.

3

Twenty-four hours later, on July 18, Citizen King gave his consent. Most of that night, amidst billowing smoke from burning stores and ricocheting pistol reports in the darkness, I hastily loaded the trunk of my battered old Chevelle with cardboard boxes of film and files about the Movement and the minister. Amy agreed with King that it would be best to separate Smith from the city for a while. Removing him far from his old haunts, the locations that reminded him of his losses, might be just the caisson required for restoring his life. Downstate, in rural Jackson County (fondly called Little Egypt by locals who'd named their hot, dusty towns Cairo and Thebes after Old Testament cities), a few miles from Makanda, Mama Pearl owned a hundred-year-old farmhouse handed down from her father. For two weeks that would be, as Amy called it, our Nest.

Provided we escaped the South Side in one piece.

The riot's devastation spread over 140 blocks, spilling into Slumdale, and we had to get across town to Smith's room. The minister was now on the West Side, preaching brotherhood and peaceful revolution on streets that ran slick with blood. Black blood, as if in the city (any city) ritual acts of murder had to be repeated night after night to renew the city itself. I feared the fires might burn forever, akin to brimstone, for the influence of the neocolonial empire King so relentlessly criticized stretched from Southeast Asia to Rhodesia, Colombia to Watts. One block from the minister's place, the police were shoving women and children into paddy wagons. Teenagers tossed Molotov cocktails at squad cars. At the corner of Sixteenth two white patrolmen weighted down by duty-belts chased a black teenager in blue jeans and a baseball cap through clouds of tear gas eerily backlit by the blaze from a torched pawnshop. Looters spilled from the building, hauling away portable Motorola televisions, shotguns, bolt-action rifles, and radios piled high in wobbly-wheeled shopping carts.

When the boy slipped on broken glass from the store's shattered window the cops fell upon him, cracking his bones with a flurry of blows I felt echo through my own body. My stomach clenched. Spotting another looter, the cops took off, leaving the boy bleeding on the sidewalk. As in a dream, I watched myself running toward the spot where the boy lay rocking back and forth, his legs drawn up to his chest. He was blinded by blood streaming into his eyes. Teeth hung loose in his head. "Don't move," I said. "Let me help you, brother." I reached down, holding out my right hand so the boy could rise. Without warning, he kicked straight up at my knees, bringing me crashing to the sidewalk. I felt blows falling across my face, breaking my glasses. He buried his shoe in my stomach. I felt his fingers snaking through my pockets, emptying them of my wallet, keys, coins. I thought, *All right, now he's finished.* But I was wrong. He began kicking me again, intent on killing me for the thrill of it. I could barely see, but I crawled to the curb, pulling myself along the glass-sprinkled concrete to a parked car, and rolled under it, only to feel his fingers tighten on my right ankle. He pulled me back into the open, bringing his heel down on my back. I knew then I was going to die. Just another casualty of the night's rioting. I saw him reach behind his back into the waistband of his trousers, and as if by magic a gleaming switchblade appeared in his hand, which he raised high above his head, his eyes glittering to slits as he chose the spot on my chest where he would bury the blade. Then, miraculously, I heard a crack like wood snapping cartilage. The boy cried out. Moments later, he was gone, blending back into the night, replaced by Chaym Smith, who stood above me, breathing heavily and holding a two-by-four he'd found in the street and shouting for me to give him my keys and get in the car before we all were mistaken for rioters and rounded up with the rest.

"Thank you—"

"*Sama-sama.*"

"What?"

"I said you're welcome, in Indonesian. Just get in the goddamn car, Bishop."

"Chaym . . . if you hadn't stopped him—"

"Uh-hunh, I know. You'd be dead. C'mon, let's go."

Smith slid over from the passenger side to the driver's seat and hunched over the wheel. Still shaken, unable to keep my hands from trembling, I gathered my things off the pavement and climbed in back behind Amy, who was holding a shopping bag full of King's old clothing. I fumbled through my coat, hoping I still had the three- by four-inch copy of the King James Bible, a gift long ago from my mother, which I carried as a kind of talisman for times of trouble, or just to study when I rode the subway. Not that I really felt much anymore when I fingered the Book's tissue-thin pages. Try as I might, I no longer could breathe life into the vision the Bible embodied—or, for that matter, into any system of meaning, though I desperately wanted to, and always kept the Book nearby out of habit, often just letting its pages wing open to a passage selected by chance, hoping someday it would speak to me again.

Amy turned round in her seat and removed my glasses, which were dangling off my face, then took one of the minister's handkerchiefs and held it against the fresh cuts on my forehead. "Oh, Matthew," she groaned, "why didn't you stay by the car?"

"Yeah," said Smith, "you're lucky I decided not to wait for you and came on my own. You *owe* me one, Bishop. Don't forget that. And what the hell d'you think you were doing anyway?"

"I was just trying to help," I said. "He probably thought I was the police coming back."

"Sure," said Smith, "that's why he was cleaning out your pockets, right?" He laughed wickedly. "Guys like you got a lot to learn. You really do. Good thing you weren't in Korea with me. The enemy just loved would-be missionary types like you. Know what those crafty bastards would do if five of us were out on patrol? They'd wound two Yanks, knowin' that'd end the fight because it would take three men to get the injured back to the base. And we *had* to get them back, bein' Americans and Christians and all that. They counted on it. They saw it as a weakness that we couldn't leave our own behind. And you know what else I saw, Bishop? You know what they'd do when they killed a black soldier and a white one? They'd cut off their heads, put the white one on the black man's body and the black one on the white boy. It was a *joke*, okay? I saw that, and it showed me there's two kinds of people in this world. Predators and prey. Lions and *lunch*. You see it any other way, buddy, and people will chump you off." He glanced back at the little book I held. "If you'd been through half of what I have, you'd put that Bible away and learn what time it is—or learn how to read it *right*."

"That's unfair," said Amy. "Matthew was just trying to help that boy."

"Yeah, and you *saw* what happened. Some people can't be helped. I know that. You reach down to pull somebody up, he's liable to drag you down to the bottom with him, then spit on you to boot. Did I hear you call him *brother*?" Smith chortled, his head tipping back. "You didn't even know his name! Did you call him that 'cause he was black, or was that a church thing? You ever *thought* about what brothers are really like? Romulus and Remus, say. Or Jacob and Esau? How they can hate each other, especially if one is doing better? See, if I were you, I'd forget about that brotherhood malarkey, and remember what they said during the French Revolution. *Fraternité ou la mort*. What I'm saying—and you may not like this—is that in the Struggle, *who* you are is less important than *what* you are: a splib, an outcast united to others by oppression, by blood, and let me tell you, buddy, that's one frail, forced confederacy, with some *brothers* and *sisters* who can be downright scary when they want to close ranks against the racist enemy, some of 'em all but saying, *Be my brother or I'll kill you!*"

"No," Amy said, shocked. "How can you say that? I thought you said you wanted to preach."

"What'd you think I was just doing?"

"I mean, *be* a right and proper minister!"

"Oh . . . well, I did. Once."

55

"What about now? Last night you talked differently. You were almost begging for help. But tonight you don't sound like the same person at all. Which are you?"

Smith was quiet, his hands squeezed round the steering wheel at nine and three o'clock. Then he rummaged through his trouser pocket, found a linty, flecked stick of Doublemint gum, and stuck the wad into his cheek. "Sometimes I don't know," he said. "Maybe you can help me figure that out." He looked sheepishly at her. "I'm sorry, I guess I didn't know what I was saying. It's been like that since I was at Elgin. Can you forgive me?"

At that Amy softened. Her profile from where I sat dissolved from irritation to sympathy, as if it was the minister himself who'd appealed to her for understanding, seeing how he'd looked in a flickerflash trompe l'oeil uncannily like King when he apologized. For an instant I could have sworn Smith was playing her masterfully like a finely tuned lyre, one keyed to her (all of our) affection for King, fluidly shifting from one mask to another as the occasion demanded, as if maybe the self was a fiction—or, if not that, a multiplicity of often conflicting profiles. He seemed full of Machiavellian deceits and subterfuges. To my astonishment, he glided from the tribal languages of the Academy to Niggerese, a skill a most educated black men possessed (myself included), but in Smith's hands, black slang became a weapon used for startling effect, like tossing a grenade into the middle of a polite tea party. As he put rubber to the road, tear gas drifted into the car, the shock of inhaling it like breathing in burning coals or hellfire when it filled the tissues of my lungs. I pressed one hand over my mouth, but I couldn't breathe or see. Smith gave more gas to the Chevelle, gunning it through an intersection, the speedometer riding sixty, then he stomped on the brake and began to skid. Up ahead, an elderly barefoot black man, wearing only wrinkled blue pajamas, held his bloody forehead and stepped blindly into the beam of the Chevelle's headlights. Smith cut the wheel hard, running the car onto the sidewalk. A mailbox sprang up in the way, and he cranked the wheel again, passing just close enough to throw gravel against the man's kneecaps but leaving him otherwise untouched as the car slammed through another intersection and at last came to rest in front of Smith's building.

Amy was shaking. "You almost *hit* that man!"

"Fool shouldn'ta been out." Smith rolled his window down, now that the tear gas was behind us, and coughed. "Let's get my things. It won't take long, I don't have that much."

Actually, it would take less time than he knew. All of Smith's belongings were piled on the street and stairs in front of 3721 Indiana Avenue. "I don't believe this," he whispered. On the sidewalk his shoulders slumped; he looked from his possessions dumped like refuse up to his landlady's third-floor window. He climbed the stair, favoring his left leg, whipped out his key, and stuck it about a quarter-inch into the door before it stopped. He twisted it once. Twice, then it broke off in his hand. "She *did* it," he was still whispering, staring at the fragment on his palm. "Mrs. Thomas locked me out . . ."

"It's all right," said Amy. "We can put some of this in Matthew's car and come back later."

Smith threw his key into the street and headed for the rear of the building. "Do what you want with it."

"Wait! Where are you going?"

"Got some business to tend to. I'll be back."

After he disappeared into the alley, Amy glanced at me, shrugged, then began loading Smith's belongings into the trunk and backseat. I moved to help, handing her a framed photograph of two young black servicemen so fit their uniforms seemed molded to their muscular frames, both grinning toward the camera, one of them (Smith, I was sure) holding up two fingers like rabbit ears behind the head of a friend I guessed was Stackhouse; and I found several paintings, one canvas portraying Jesus as a work-toughened carpenter, rendered (Amy told me) in the style of G. Bierman's *The Ascension*; another—a watercolor in the manner of Kawase Hasui—depicted an ancient temple all but hidden by jungle growth and was entitled *Borobudur*, while a third showed a sparsely furnished hospital room in Elgin as van Gogh might have imagined it, and in the last I saw a young black woman with three good-looking boys done in the vein of a Matisse. I stared at these paintings for the longest time, lost in them, startled by Smith's talent, his shape-shifting ability to change styles as rapidly as others changed their garments, and then Amy was telling me to hurry up, so I moved on, passing to her some shoes eaten away at the soles, slacks and shirts so old they could only have come from rummage sales or Goodwill; there were a few dented pots and pans, a battered saxophone, a worn Bible with notecards inserted throughout its pages, sandals made of rice straw, a straight razor, a cloth bag with Chinese characters I could not read, a wicker hat, a Smith & Wesson .357 (Model 27), a seven-inch Army knife in its stiff leather sheath, and wrapped in a quilted blanket a shabby black robe and a tatami mat. Judging by the cardboard boxes at my feet, whatever Smith lacked in clothing he more than made up for in books. There were volumes from Moody Bible Institute, translations from the Coptic Gnostic Library (unearthed in 1945 near the town of Nag Hammadi in Upper Egypt), the Rhineland sermons of Meister Eckhart, the Dhammapada, texts on the Sufi and Tantrism, and on their front pages, in their margins, he had scribbled his commentaries in a script so small, so microscopic, it might have come from the hand of a mathematician. In other boxes I found Japanese pornography—magazines with page upon glossy page of photos showing teenagers (some of them dressed as schoolgirls) doing things I dare not describe, but which I guessed he used for masturbation, and then!—I saw playing cards depicting a different, more terrifying kind of pornography: Thai pictures taken in morgues, showing bodies in different stages of decomposition, used by Theravada monks for meditation on the transitory nature of all things.

With each box and shopping bag of Smith's things I found myself falling through his past and into passageways of a constantly mutating soul which, I'd wager, even his therapists at Elgin had not fully charted. Poking through a shopping bag, I pulled out expired passports stamped by half the countries left of Hawaii, a sketchbook filled with his poetry and drawings—penciled images of well-known locations in the Loop, and possible portraits of what his own father might look like (one was a derelict feeding himself from a Dumpster, another was Daddy King)—hypodermic needles I was afraid to handle, and eight scrapbooks in which he'd pasted news articles about, I thought, himself. I looked again. These were stories about King, some of them dating back to the Montgomery bus boycott. He'd saved everything—from the *Time* magazine "Man of the Year" cover story on King to cartoonist Mort Drucker's satire of the Movement in *Mad* magazine. Smith had flagged the numerous articles critical of King, as if he took a delicious pleasure in publicity that diminished the man he so resembled and clearly revered.

I was dazed, staring at these pages, when he came back, sweating, with the scent of gasoline on his clothes. Climbing into the car, he said, "We got to go. Right *now*."

"We're not finished," I said. "We're still loading your things."

"Forget them! We got to go *now*."

Dropping one of the boxes, I climbed in. I cranked the starter as Amy closed the trunk and got in the back, then I eased out into the street. Smith grumbled, "Keep driving," so I floored the pedal and headed south. In my rearview mirror I saw smoke billowing from his building on Indiana Avenue.

Smith grinned.

"Chaym—"

"Don't look back." He stretched out and closed his eyes for the six-hour, three-hundred-mile trip downstate. "Musta been the rioters done that. Gonna try to get some rest."

Amy kicked off her leather sandals, then curled up in a corner of the backseat, her head pillowed on one of the bags from Smith's apartment. All the way to Champaign I drove in silence broken only by news reports on the radio. During the night National Guardsmen had clanked into the city like centurions to reinforce local police. The mayor's office placed blame for the devastation on King's presence in Chicago. Listening to that newscast, I found it easy to conclude there was precious little light in politics, which, I remembered, Henry Adams had called the "systematic organization of hatreds." King's efforts in Chicago had pried open a Pandora's box of racial paradoxes, not the least being that in the wake of Black Power's appeal in the northern ghettos his political approach was unraveling at the seams. Like so many who admired the King of 1963, the piecemeal reformist Daley championed his success in Selma, but along with his six black aldermen who controlled wards on the South and West sides, he would not concede to the anticapitalist King of 1966 that his city was a bastion of bigotry based on economic exploitation. On local television, Rev. Joseph H. Jackson pointed out to the minister that Chicago had problems but was not the Deep South. Furthermore, some said, the objectives of the Movement were hazy. Many blacks wondered if one of the fundamental goals of freedom should be the chance to live next door to white people in places like Cicero and Hyde Park. To be sure, the SCLC proved housing discrimination by sending black allies to real estate agents, who steered them away from properties they eagerly sold later that same afternoon to whites. But could a family living on $4,000 a year afford a home with a view of Lake Michigan in Winnetka? King's critics dismissed the battle for that sort of integration as bourgeois. And for all the riveting drama of the minister's previous campaigns, his desperate bid at sparking a fire of social change in America's second-largest city, and regaining the reins of the Movement from modern-day Zealots eager to pick up the gun, led only that July to men and women foot-weary from marching and fires in the streets that gutted only the black ghetto. The minister traveled by police escort (many derided that) to bars, churches, and meeting halls, begging angry black crowds to replace violence with mass action aimed at disruption, sending the city officials a collective Thoreauvian *no* to institutionalized inequality.

Yet I wondered if the legal and histrionic tactics of the Movement might one day prove more costly than anyone imagined. One could not hold a referendum for racial justice in America, a vote, because—as everyone knew—whites would surely cast their ballots for, at best, gradual change. And in the South for no change at all. What the nation needed in the early 1960s was to be electrified by having the evils at its core uncovered. The minister was a master at that. And at enlisting the powers of the federal government to accelerate the end of American apartheid. But I wondered: Would the wounds uncovered ever heal? At times I felt uncomfortable with the SCLC's and NAACP's reliance, their dependency and complete faith in Washington's clout, the protection it offered black people—but at what price? Nothing, my mother once told me, came without a price; there was always a trade-off of some kind, even though one might not see it clearly in the beginning. Mightn't whites come to perceive Negroes as no longer a victimized class but a privileged one, thus leading to a resentment and a lack of respect and racial disdain greater than anything witnessed during the era of Jim Crow? Mightn't too much reliance on the federal government, even in private affairs such as rearing a family, lead to the inability to do for oneself, unhampered by bad laws, that was the Movement's original purpose?

I switched channels and found an all-music station playing the Supremes, then looked back at Amy. She slept with one finger brushing her lips, and as I looked at her I felt lost. Brown freckles ran right across her nose, and since she lay facing the east, sunlight brought out highlights in her hair. She seemed to grow quieter and sleep more deeply with each county we put between ourselves and the dislocating spirit of the city. Back there, her apartment had five locks on the door. On top of that, she lived in a section of town so crime-ridden that she was obliged to padlock every door inside too. It was a frightful way to live, in fear, barricaded behind your door each evening, wondering if a neighbor might kill you in your sleep, and it was that dreadful situation the minister hoped to change.

I knew his odds were bad.

The nonviolent Movement drew successfully from the ranks of the black middle class, students at Fisk, and liberal whites in its early days, but stalled and sputtered in poor, grassroots communities. King himself subjected it to this criticism, saying voting rights and integrated lunch counters cost the nation nothing. The new campaign—class struggle—would indeed be costly. Yet over and over he insisted that the Movement needed to wage war on two fronts. First, changing the souls of men so that they not only protested for peace but in themselves *were* peace embodied, loving in even life's smallest affairs. And, second, he called for changing society so the soul might have a field in which to flourish. Neither front, he said, could be ignored, for one reinforced the other. Tremendous effort had gone into the second theater of battle, I thought. Far less into the first. So little, in fact, that as I steered south through the land of Lincoln, down a steaming highway dotted with roadkill between Springfield and Centralia, as Amy and Smith slept, my thoughts reached back to a speech the earlier "reformist" King delivered in Chicago, one that challenged and chided me when I was a freshman at Columbia College in 1964. That speech had looked inward, not out. It emphasized being fully alive in the present, which I found appealing, because didn't dwelling on the Promised Land or heaven or the Workers' Paradise postpone full immersion in life to the distant future, so that since the Civil War black people could never be at peace in the present, comfortable with the past, and were waiting, always waiting, for a day of redemption that forever receded like the horizon? Two years earlier King had not spoken that way. He'd said, "When you are behind in a foot race, the only way to get ahead is to run faster than the man in front of you. So when your white roommate says he's tired and goes to sleep, you stay up and burn the midnight oil." He spoke from experience, having maintained only a 2.48 grade point average at Morehouse College; by the time he left Crozer Seminary he was student body president and class valedictorian. He talked of his father—who, like old Joe Kennedy, was not an easy father to have—a poor, barely literate boy whose grandfather Jim Long had been used by his master to breed slaves; Daddy King often said, "I came from nowhere." At age fifteen, he could read but not write. Just the same, determination to win the hand of a Spelman seminary student named Alberta Williams, and to rise in Atlanta's black world, riveted him to study, "until I was falling asleep saying my lessons to myself."

But Chaym Smith was clearly not Daddy King. And he, Amy, and I were the most unlikely of teams with a task so impossible that the thought of it kept my Protestant stomach perpetually cramped, knotted, and queasy from the moment King asked us to work together.

Beside me, Smith—our Melchizedek—dozed. I noticed that the muscles around his mouth and eyes had relaxed, and for the time he was submerged in himself, in that depthless place of dreamless sleep where we spend a third of our lives, he looked serene, almost cherubic, the contours of his cheeks rounded, all the tension in his normally furrowed brow gone, as if a fire somewhere in him had been extinguished. In dreamless sleep, a king was not a king, nor a pauper poor; no one was old or young, male or female, cursed or blessed, educated or ignorant, sinner or saint. (And even in our dreams, there was no apartheid, no segregation between black and white.) This was the face, very Apollonian, I associated most closely with the minister in old photos I'd seen of him when he was a boy who loved to sing "I Want to Be More and More Like Jesus" and sat rapt with attention behind the pulpit of Atlanta's Ebenezer Church and his father stood ramrod straight, preaching with one finger pointed toward heaven. Or in other pictures from 1951 when he happily posed, like a prince who knew a great kingdom awaited him, beside the stately presence of his mother, with just the slightest sprinkling of pimples on his forehead and one lone pustule on his left cheek. Smith awoke, caught me glancing sideways at him, and smirked.

"Like what you see, eh?"

"I'm sorry," I said. "I didn't mean to stare. It's just that you look so much like him. Yet you're so different. Chaym, I didn't know you were a painter—"

"Yeah," he yawned, now looking very Dionysian. "I painted some when I was institutionalized. The doctors thought it'd help me heal. As you can see, I ain't no famous beauty, nobody's gonna mistake me for Harry Belafonte, but I was hoping that if I created something beautiful, I could offer that to others. Something that would live after I was gone. A li'l piece of me, you know, that'd endure. Problem was, I was second-rate. Naw, I didn't say bad. What I did— *every*thing I've done—was good. Thing is, being just good don't get you to heaven. And I'm just too mediocre for hell. God don't like near misses. Runner-ups and also-rans. Second-best means no banana. Purgatory, I been thinkin', was designed for people like me . . . and you."

"Me?"

"That's right. Who's your daddy?"

"I . . . don't know."

"That's what I figured. You like most of the rest of us. Brothers, I mean. You're illegitimate. No father prepared the way for you. You want to be among the anointed, the blessed—to *belong*. I saw that in you the moment we met. Nothing's worked for you, I can see that. You ain't never gonna have fame or fortune. Maybe not even a girl. I'll bet you ain't had pussy since pussy had you. When you die, it'll be like you never lived. That's why I said I think I can help you."

"With *what*?"

"Your salvation," he said. "You work real hard at being good, Bishop. Anybody can see you're a Boy Scout. Square as a Necker's cube. But you don't fit. You got to remember that nobody on earth likes Negroes. Not even Negroes. We're outcasts. And outcasts can't never create a community. I been to a lot of places and it's the same everywhere. We're despised worldwide. You ever thought we might be second-class citizens because generally we *are* second-rate?"

I almost slammed on the brakes. "Excuse me?"

"You heard me right. You got to face up to the fact of black—or human—mediocrity damned near across the board. Outside of entertainment and athletics (just another kind of entertainment), we don't count for shit, boy. Ain't you never felt that being a Negro means you always got the guilty suspicion you done something wrong but you ain't sure what? And don't blame it on bigotry. Nobody believes that tired old excuse anymore. What you got to face, Bishop—hey, watch the road, you're swerving—is the possibility that we are, as a tribe, descended from the first of two brothers whose best just couldn't hack it. And, it wasn't *his* fault. See, if you check that Bible of yours, you'll find the world didn't begin with love. It kicked off with killing and righteous hatred and *ressentiment*. Envy, I'm saying, *is* the Negro disease. We got the stain, the mark. Nothing else really explains our situation, far as I can see."

It took all my strength to keep from driving right off the road. "That's insane, it's certifiably mad—"

"I been that, sure. Got the papers to prove it. I *was* crazy as a coot after what happened to Juanita and her kids. But not now. I've been on the *outside* long enough to know that hatred is healthy—even holy—and that until you step away, or they cast you out, you can't see nothin' clearly. Truth is, being on the outside is a blessing. Naw, it's a necessity, if you got any creative spark at all. You know Husserl's *epoché*, what that does? No"—he squinted at me—"you probably don't. And that's too bad, 'cause the way I see it, the problem with all the fuckin' anointed and somebody like Abel—his name, according to Philo, means 'one who refers all things to God'—is that they're sheep. That's right, part of the obedient, tamed, psalm-singing herd. They make me sick, every one of 'em. See, I ain't never been good at group-think. You ever notice how safe and dull and correct they all are? How

66

timid! And unoriginal? How vulgar and materialistic? Call 'em what you want, Christians or Communists or Cultural Nationalists, but I call 'em sheep. Or zombies—that's what Malcolm X called the Nation of Islam, you know, after he broke away from Elijah, *his* surrogate daddy. There's not a real individual in the bunch. No risk-takers, Bishop. No iconoclasts. Nobody who thinks the unthinkable, or is cursed (or blessed) with bearing the cross of a unique, singular identity . . . except for him." He paused, kneading his lower lip between his forefinger and thumb; he was thinking, I guessed, of the minister. "Individuality . . . That scares 'em. In Japan, they got a saying: the nail that sticks up gets hammered down. You see what I'm saying? What's the goal after integration? Shopping at Saks Fifth Avenue? Is that what so many civil rights workers died for? Me, I ain't studyin' 'bout integrating with no run-of-the-mill white folks, or black ones either. But that's how you get to belong, boy—by fitting in and mumbling the party line and keeping your head down and losing your soul, but I think I can save you from that if you let me."

I couldn't believe he was saying these things; I wondered if he meant them (which I couldn't believe) or if he was playing with me simply to see what I'd say. I mean, the minister had instructed me to help *him*. At that moment I couldn't see him as mad. No, I saw him as wicked. Yet he made me recall the minister's sermon "Transformed Nonconformist," wherein he railed against the "mass mind," the cowardice of the herd, and proclaimed, "Any Christian who blindly accepts the opinions of the majority and in fear and timidity follows a path of expediency and social approval is a mental and spiritual slave."

I said, "Who *are* you?"

"I dunno," Smith replied. "I'm always findin' that out. I guess I make it up as I go along. Pull off there, I got to pee."

I flicked the turn signal and coasted the car off the highway toward a tiny, two-pump station and diner that must have dated back to the Depression. A low, barrel-roofed building, it squatted in the shadow of an abandoned red-brick warehouse. The sign blazoned in black letters across its front said PIT STOP. The exterior, faded green and yellow, looked weathered and washed out in the bright midday sunlight. Taped to one of the diner's cloudy windows was a cardboard sign announcing the day's special (DELUXE STEAK SANDWICH—$1.75) beside a campaign poster promoting a Republican candidate for the state senate.

"Matthew," said Amy, starting to wake, "why're we stopping here?"

"I gotta piss," said Smith, "and I'm hungry."

Squinting at the Pit Stop, knuckling both her eyes, she said, "I think I'll wait in the car."

Smith stepped out, gravel crunching under his shoe. Every ancient warning signal in my head from childhood told me to stay in the car. But I was hungry too. Parked off to one side of the diner was a rust-eaten pickup truck with a gun rack, an English setter tied in the bed, and a GOLDWATER FOR PRESIDENT sticker on the rear bumper. The dog started barking the moment I shut off the engine, which rattled for a while, then coughed and finally stuttered to a stop.

I stepped from the Chevelle into a hot shower of sunlight and moved, stiff-rumped and sore, through blistering air toward the door. My heart drew tight. I slowed my step, and stopped Smith at the door.

"Chaym . . . I think we should go somewhere else."

He arched his back, stretching. "What's the matter? You afraid they won't serve us? *You* go somewhere else. I'm starvin', and I know my rights."

He stepped inside, his head rammed forward, and I followed, my eyes taking only a moment to adjust to the dark, low-ceilinged interior. I began a prayer but the words did not come. The air inside the diner was soured by the smell of grease. Over the stove the ceiling was smoke-grimed, and beneath our feet the once-brown linoleum was scuffed and faded. Five small booths, darkened by use, ran the length of the diner on my right. Slut's wool had been swept into the corners. A portable fan blew hot air across a long, curving counter. There, an old man, thin and balding and wearing round black-rimmed bifocals clamped over the bulb of his waxy nose, sat on a leather stool, reading an edition of the *St. Louis Post-Dispatch* that headlined the riot in Chicago. His fingernails were dark with dirt, his chin seemed to drop straight into his neck, the back of which was hacked and leathery, and his overalls hung loose in the crotch. On the other side of the counter a middle-aged woman shaped like the Venus of Willendorf, with hazel eyes in a flat, pale face enveloped by red-blond hair, was topping off his cup with black coffee. The name stitched over the pocket of her stained uniform read ARLENE. When Smith entered they both stopped suddenly and stared. Just stared, as if he and I were spacemen who'd fallen from the stars.

"You bet' be open for business now," said Smith. "We come a long way . . ."

Arlene's head made an infinitesimal bob, but she was still pouring steaming hot coffee—beyond the rim of the old man's cup and along the porcelain counter, where it spilled onto his narrow lap and squeezed a whoop out of him that so startled her the pot fell clattering from her fingers to the floor. She scrambled to clean up the mess. Smith made a nasty chuckle, relishing every moment of confusion our appearance had caused.

"You hear what I said?" he asked. "Can we get served?"

Arlene was still staring. "I guess I can wait on you." She had one of those roosterish, unmusical American voices, coarsened by years of smoking Camel straights, full of cracks and cackle. "The owner, he's not here. Are you . . ."

"Am I what?"

She pointed toward the newspaper in front of the old man, who was swabbing his wet crotch with a fistful of napkins, to a front-page, above-the-crease photograph of King in a Chicago poolroom surrounded by admiring teenagers as he leaned over the green felt of a pool table, lining up the cue for his shot. Arlene said, "Him. Is that *you*?"

"No." Abruptly, he was very quiet.

"Really? You look just like him."

"I'm *not* him," Smith said angrily, and the saying of it seemed to knock the wind out of him, as if he'd been asked that a thousand times, and each time whoever asked was disappointed, making him feel like an impostor, less than the real McCoy. He lifted one of the leather-bound menus stacked on the counter next to displays of candy and fresh pies, and studied it as the old man, dripping, scurried out. Arlene continued to gawk at us.

"I want four specials for me'n my friends, to go. You got a bathroom here?"

"Outside, around the back. You know, I almost asked for your autograph—"

"You still want it?"

"Well, if you were *him*, I might, but—"

Smith walked out before she finished.

Arlene blinked, pushing a limp, lawless lock of hair, dampened by the heat, off her forehead with the back of her hand. "Did I say something wrong?"

"No," I said, "he's just sensitive about his looks."

"Well, the way he left, you'd think I called him a name. He *does* look like that colored preacher, the one causin' all the big to-do up in Chicago. I wanted his autograph 'cause he's in the paper all the time, but that don't mean I like how he's stirrin' things up. I get along with colored just fine, but that Dr. Coon—"

"King." My stomach heaved. "His name is King."

"Whatever, I just think he's pushin' things too fast." She took a deep breath. "You go 'head and sit down. I can serve you since you're gonna take it out. I'll have your order in a minute."

She stepped to the freezer, took out four hamburger patties that looked as if they'd just thrown off a lingering illness, and dropped them into a skillet on the grill. My belly was still knotted. I'd wanted to slap her, but I remembered how my mother told me to behave in public, and how polite and civilized and patient the minister was himself—always a credit to the race—when confronting white people with an I.Q. the size of their shoes. I tried not to hate her. At the spot where she'd been leaning on the counter when we entered there was a copy of a movie star magazine beside a pack of cigarettes and an ashtray packed with butts bearing the imprint of incisors I'd noticed were stained brown by nicotine when she opened her mouth. In fact, she'd tried to keep her hand over her mouth when speaking to conceal an overbite and the tartar and decay on her front teeth. With her back to the counter, I could see a blemish on her neck from cheap, dimestore jewelry.

I closed my eyes, both hands resting on my lap. Smith's words in the car ran through my head, then the memory of trips my mother and I made to visit relatives in South Carolina when I was young fell through my heart like rain. I remembered roadside cafés like this diner, where we stopped hungry and tired after seven hours of driving and were told we could be served only if we went to the back entrance. Another image rose up: badly lit department stores near my relatives' homes in Abbeville where they enjoyed the privilege of purchasing clothes like other citizens from the pale, blond salesgirls but could not try them on their bodies before the sale was made, as if their skin was unclean, corrupt in some way, and might contaminate or blemish with the ancient stain of blackness these cheap garments off the rack. All this my mother accepted, and she never corrected the teenage employees when they called her "girl," which even then made my thoughts turn murderous with hate and humiliation, as an incident King experienced in 1944 brought him "perilous close" to despising white people when during his college days he was seated behind a curtain on a dining car, a shade pulled down to obliterate entirely the offensiveness of his presence. And so he rode behind a screen, trapped within their ideas of his identity, his blood pressure soaring, which meant even his health and the risk of myocardial infarction was at the mercy of people he despised, and he could do no more to change this than my mother who, dragging me in tow, tramped through mud around the café to the kitchen door, where we waited for what seemed hours, listening to the laughter and voices of customers and the clatter of dishes and silverware inside. I remembered that my mother's expression was sad but stoic as she looked into the distance with her chin lifted, both hands folded in front of her, and I saw that for me she would suffer a thousand indignities and denials of her personhood so that I would not go hungry, dying this way every day, one little piece at a time, in order to wrest from the world not great victories but the most pathetically simple items for survival—hand-me-down clothes from the women whose houses she cleaned and the plate of food wrapped in foil the café's waitress at last brought to us, handing it to my mother with a self-satisfied smile as if she'd done something good and noble that day, a compassionate deed her pastor would praise come Sunday, because she had not turned us away but instead fed the coloreds, the grendels, through the back door, not cast us out as some would, which was unchristian, but consigned us to a more benign phantom realm east of Eden where we were, if not fully human, half-men and half-women: poor, damned creatures scratching at her kitchen door like cats for a bowl of milk. (Wasn't that how JFK had once described blacks, as "poor bastards"?) And for this meal, this phantom nourishment, my mother gave her money, said *God bless you*—I remember her blessing them—then back inside her car as we continued south she made me eat every morsel for which she had so dearly paid.

Arlene placed our food on the counter, her lips compressed, as Smith came back from the bathroom, and rang up the bill. "That's four dollars and fifty cents."

I handed her a five-dollar bill. She placed it in the cash register, then scooped out my change. I thrust my palm toward her for the coins, and had perfect control of myself, the magnanimity and external calm my mother had insisted upon, and which the Movement's leaders so nobly embodied, until she slapped the money on the counter, and something inside me (I don't know what) snapped (I don't know how), flooding me with a hatred so hot, like a drug, I was nearly blinded by it as I threw the food in her face, hurled from the counter sugar canisters and ketchup bottles smashing against the wall behind the grill, screaming so loud and long my glasses steamed; then, as Arlene fled toward the rear of the diner, I stormed outside to the car, Smith right at my heels.

He was grinning. "Very nice. You were vicious, Bishop. I think your best line was calling her an insignificant, execrable bitch mired in the booboisie—that's from Mencken, right?"

"I said that?"

"Oh, yeah," he cackled. "And more. You left her toasted, roasted, and with an apple in her mouth. It was choice. You

73

sounded like William F. Buckley on bad acid. I always *knew* it'd be sweet to see a black intellectual go ballistic."

I was shaking too badly to drive. And I felt ashamed, as if I'd failed the minister, my mother, myself. I gave Smith my keys—his smile mashed his cheeks up in parallel moons—and within a few minutes we were back on the highway, heading farther south. For the longest time I sat with my hands squeezed between my knees, my fists clenched, afraid that at any moment I'd see in the rearview mirror a highway patrol car pulling up behind us, yet I felt exhilarated by what I'd done.

Smith kept grinning at me, happily patting out rhythms on the steering wheel with his palms. "You all right." He reached over and patted my shoulder. "With a li'l more work, you gonna love it where *I* live."

4

There were many times when he wondered if he was wrong.

Sitting by the window in the second row of first-class seats, all the others empty at this hour, on the predawn flight that shuttled him back and forth between Chicago and Atlanta, where he was determined to earn his $6,000-a-year salary by delivering a sermon each Sunday, he thought back to the astonishing victories granted him by the Lord of Love, and forward to the November retreat planned for his staff at which time he felt he should remind them how he was still searching and did not have all the answers. Nonviolence, he felt, was an experiment with truth. It was a truth-seeking process. That was all in this world he could say with certainty . . .

It was four-thirty in the morning. The engines of the airplane roared around him as it tore down the runway, shaking loose poorly secured doors on the overhead compartments and, behind him, throwing dishes to the floor in the tiny cubicle that served as a galley. That so much metal could even leave the ground and stay airborne always startled and delighted him (and in single-engine planes, in which he refused to ride, terrified him). Airplanes piqued his anagogic and analogical side, the old student of Aquinas who enjoyed reasoning vertically from the natural world toward heaven, which these flying machines came close to bumping into. Unconsciously he pressed his feet forward under the seat in front of him to keep his small black suitcase from sliding into the aisle, though if it spilled open there would be little to retrieve because he felt best when he traveled light with as little baggage as possible, physical and metaphysical. Toward the front of the plane, beneath the red FASTEN SEAT BELTS and NO SMOKING signs, the black stewardess who'd brought coffee and a pillow and fussed over him when he boarded was strapping herself into a bucket seat that folded out of the wall. She'd told him her name was Stephanie. An Alabaman raised to value the goodwill and hospitality that was so much a part of his own upbringing, she'd asked for his autograph and couldn't do enough for him. Apparently, she'd seen his name on the passenger list, then rushed out and purchased forty copies of Stride Toward Freedom, inserting in each one the inscription she wanted him to write for her family and friends. "I hope you won't mind," she'd said. He saw the cardboard box of books at her feet, and sighed. All he wanted to do was work on his sermon and nap before they arrived in Atlanta. She couldn't know how sensitive he was about people fawning over him, or how every worldly honor he received (he had more medals than a Russian general) threw him into the deepest reflection on whether he deserved these distinctions and if one day they'd prove to be more weight than they were worth. Glorifying any man was a sin. But he accepted the honors so as not to offend. People sent him photos of their newborns named after him, their wedding snapshots, and constantly wrote him requests for his auto-graphed portrait. Always he or someone on his staff responded. After his trip to India he'd vowed to set aside one day a week for fasting and meditation, and to spend more time in study— he was certain he needed these things to be a better leader. Yet there never seemed to be enough time to keep those vows . . . Their eyes caught across the cabin. Stephanie was smiling at him again, then she winked and looked back at the clipboard on her lap.

Suddenly he felt warm. With two fingers he pulled loose the tight knot of his tie, undid the top button on his shirt, then pushed up the window's stiff curtain at his right, peering down at blinking lights on the plane's silvery deltoid wing, and beyond that to the waters of Lake Michigan. The sun, huge and liquid, hung over the horizon. From this height waves wimpling the blue surface looked frozen, as if someone had called time out on all motion in the world below, and the Wheel of Life stopped to give everyone time to catch his breath. And then he could see nothing as the plane began its steep ascent to thirty-five thousand feet—he only knew they were rising to that altitude because the pilot, a southerner by his accent, came on over the crackling loudspeaker to tell pas-sengers his flight plan and the temperature in Atlanta and to report that their crew had a combined total of fifty thousand hours in the air. Somehow the pilot's voice and experience put him at ease. Or maybe it was the vulnerability he felt when-ever he flew, knowing that someone he couldn't see or talk to had control over his destination and whether he lived or died, and most likely that person was trustworthy since his own life depended on doing his job well. It wasn't easy to be an atheist on an airplane. No sooner had you strapped in than you had to believe in something beyond yourself. Perhaps there was a ser-mon here, an exemplum he might use on Sunday. But no, afterward someone would pick it apart, like the monk Gaunilo shredding Anselm's proof for God's existence. It was too whimsical. Yet in a small way it reminded him of that terrible night in Montgomery when his faith, lukewarm since childhood, became real.

Everyone in Atlanta expected the son of the city's most influential pastor would be eager to join the church. The truth was that when he was seven, doing so was the farthest thing from his mind. But during Ebenezer's annual two-week revival in May of 1936, his sister boldly stepped forward for baptism, and this stung him sorely, the thought that Christine might get a leg up on him in anything. Halfheartedly he submitted to the ritual. But even then some critical, questioning part of him stood back, skeptical, watching himself from a distance, and mocking him a little because not only had the "crisis moment" associated with conversion eluded him but he could not square the over-the-top emotionalism of the fundamentalist Baptist church—talking in tongues and flailing on the floor when "getting happy"—with his preference for coolly and deliberately thinking things through.

Sometimes he felt at odds with others at Ebenezer. His Sunday-school teachers had little education to speak of. Nevertheless, they believed. Although none had heard of biblical hermeneutics, each old deacon and assistant pastor had been saved in that revered and awful (to him) moment of epilepsy and seizure so many said lay in wait one day for him. He told no one how that prediction cut him off at the knees after he saw a light-skinned girl from Booker T. Washington High School, one he'd been attracted to, struck down by the spirit in his father's church. Lightning seemed to single her out from the other parishioners fanning themselves and singing one of his favorite hymns, "Honor, Honor"—she was adance in the seat beside her startled mother, then it lifted her like a broken doll and flung her helplessly to the hard wooden floor. Her eyes turned up in her head. Veins in her throat stood out. There was

78

the possibility she might swallow her tongue, and that frightened him all the more and made his heart leap in his chest. He watched her wide-eyed, squeezing his hands together, as she kicked the air and tore loose her clothing, as unconscious of her nakedness as someone in one of the ancient, pre-Christian mystery cults. For months she'd ignored him. She'd been haughty, distant, in control. Now she writhed on the floor like a worm. Water ran down her legs. Her light cotton dress rose above her brown thighs, giving him an eyeful of what he'd fantasized about all summer long before the girl's mother shoved her garments down. His own mother spun him back around in his seat. Watching the girl had aroused him. Biting down hard on his knuckles, he felt burning shame shot through with the wound of desire. Spiritual hunger and sexual longing simultaneously. He closed his eyes, praying that his voyeurism, like that of Ham, had not offended the god thunderously unleashed inside the girl, yet if this violent seizure was what it meant to be saved, he hoped it would never happen to him.

He wondered if his faith was weak, if perhaps he was the worst of sinners and hypocrites. Others, he felt, suspected this too when at thirteen he shocked his teacher and classmates by rejecting the idea of Christ's bodily resurrection from the sepulcher. He questioned, he doubted the Bible's literal interpretation all through his teens, and wondered if the Negro church would ever be more Apollonian, as intellectually respectable as it was Dionysian and emotionally intense. The conflict between the intellect and emotional fervor, between the head (gnosis) and the heart (pistis), only deepened as he grew older. It held him back from following in his father's footsteps. Medicine or law, he thought, might suit him better than churches that often seemed so otherworldly they were no earthly good at all. Preparing men for heaven was all well and good. But, he wondered, what of their conditions in the here and now? Then at Morehouse his liberal professors George D.

Kelsey and Benjamin Mays gave him scholarly models for the kind of minister he one day hoped to be, filling his head with literature and philosophy, but even a jackleg preacher incapable of writing his own name had direct knowledge of the peace that passeth understanding he had only experienced in books.

During the Montgomery campaign, that ended. Threats on his life and those of Coretta and Yolanda, whom he saw too seldom at the height of the bus boycott, were nothing new. But one call shook him. It caught him, this newly minted Ph.D. whose future seemed so bright before the boycott's leadership was thrust upon him, one weary night when he came home feeling euchred and afraid his family might be snatched away. His wife was waiting by the telephone. She handed it to him. "Listen, nigger," the gin-soaked voice said, "we've taken all we want from you. Before next week you'll be sorry you ever came to Montgomery. If you aren't out of this town in three days we're gonna blow your brains out and blow up your house."

He knew he could not go on. The forces gathered against him were too many and great. Out there in the night someone was loading a 20-gauge pump-action shotgun to hunt him down; pouring gasoline into a glass jug to blow the limbs off his baby. They might be with the police. Or the military. Or Negroes displeased with all he'd stirred up. He could turn to no one for help. Not the Montgomery police, the politicians in Washington, or his parents. No one. Here, the roots of segregation ran deep, fueled by poverty. The seventy thousand whites on the average earned $1,730 yearly, the fifty thousand Negroes $970. Fewer than two thousand of the voting-age Negroes were registered, and humiliating obstacles were placed in their way. In Montgomery no Negroes held public office. The uneducated were apathetic, resigned to second-class status. The learned, especially if they belonged to any of the black civic groups, were factionalized and fought more often than they agreed.

For a long time that night he walked the floor, thinking of *Revelations* 22:15, his head tipped, both hands clenched into fists, his stomach turned to lead, searching for some way to escape his duties on the Montgomery Improvement Association without looking like a coward or a fool. Once his foot struck the leg of a table and brought a lamp and a photo of the baby bouncing onto the carpet. He swore under his breath and undid the mess he'd made. His directionless. pacing brought him into the kitchen—he could do less damage there. In order to find something to do with his trembling hands, he put a fresh pot of coffee on the stove, silently watched it brew, then slumped down with his cup at the kitchen table. Coretta was rooms away, caring for the baby. He rubbed his face with both hands. He began to heave for breath, knowing if he failed in this fight against evil, surely the others who'd sacrificed so much would falter as well. His name would be struck from the Book of Life; the boycott would unravel and nothing would have been accomplished. They would be worse off than before. Demoralized, defeated. But in heaven's name, what man could continue under this weight? He felt caged. Chained. In bondage and no longer belonging to himself. How had Boston University's rising star come to this cul-de-sac? From childhood and the days his father talked politics at the dinner table, he'd dreamed of uplifting the Race, studied and prepared himself for this great task, wanting Great Sacrifices and trials of faith only to discover, too late, that nobody—or so he feared—gave a goddamn about his bourgeois sacrifices. If Yolanda and Coretta were killed, who would care? If there was no God, as so many thinkers claimed, he was a fool for endangering his family. Love was the ontological foundation of values. God was love. It followed that without Him there could be no basis for all his appeals to justice from the pulpit. No reason for anyone to care about the poor. No argument, in the end, to counter slavery itself, for in a materialistic, mechanistic world, a neu-

tral universe onto which man projected his delusions of freedom and inherent worth, no value claims could be made at
all—the cosmos would be irrational, not benign, indifferent to
order and measure, a nightmare in the mind of some devil who
could not roll himself awake. Thus far Montgomery had shown
him that if God was not dead, He must certainly be deaf to His
people's suffering.

His fingers tightened round his empty cup until it shattered, obliterating inside and out. He took a deep breath. In
resistance to oppression, he realized, there was fear of reprisals,
in acquiescence the annihilation of self-worth, in fame the
fear of humiliation, in strength the fear of enemies, in social
stature the fear of slander, in health the fear of illness, in
beauty the fear of old age, in scholarship the fear of disputants,
in living . . . the certainty of death. His thoughts churned on,
complicated, exotic. He felt too tired to move, but his mind,
from surface to seabed, kept whirring widdershins.

At last he began to pray. To whom—or what—he could not
say. Not asking for anything then. Not fighting, only confess-
ing, "Lord, I have nothing left . . ." His gaze drifted to the fragments of the cup that was no longer a cup. But where had the
"cup" gone? His fist opened, disappearing into his hand.
Where had his "fist" gone? Then it came quietly, unbidden. He
was traveling light again, for the long, lurid dream of multiplicity and separateness, the very belief in an "I" that suffered
and strained to affect the world, dissolved, and for the first time
he felt like a dreamer gently roused from sleep and forgetful-
ness. Awake, he saw he was not the doer. How could he have
ever believed otherwise? That which he'd thought practiced
virtue, surrendered to vice, held degrees, opinions and elabo-
rated theories, and traveled toward a goal was spun from a spi-
derweb of words, no more real than the cantels of the erstwhile
cup before him. Later, he would tell reporters and his congregation the room was rayed with shadowless light, and the Lord

said unto him, Stand up for righteousness, stand up for the truth, and God will be at your side forever, *but in fact the light came from him—not without—and the* vox Dei *he heard had been his own.* Not I, *he heard it whisper again in the suddenly transparent kitchen,* but the Father within me doeth the works . . . I seek not my will but the will of the Father who sent me . . .

The stewardess's voice came over the loudspeaker. "The captain has turned off the seat-belt sign. You are free to walk around the cabin if you wish."

He struggled with the seat belt cutting into his belly and made a note to himself to push back a little earlier from banquet tables in the future. Finally the buckle sprang open, and he brought down the tray tucked into the seat in front of him. From his briefcase he removed the unfinished pages of his sermon and spread them before him, still thinking of his "Kitchen Conversion." He'd not experienced anything quite like it thereafter. Now it was a faint memory, like first love, but he knew enough to trust the Lord to remove any obstacles—himself included—placed in the way of his ministry. Needless to say, that perplexed most of his aides, the purely political ones. Again and again they told him letting God handle little details was fine at Ebenezer but if he hoped to stay at the forefront of the Movement he damned well needed to organize his campaigns better. Perhaps Chicago was proving them right. There were factors he had not foreseen. Down South the lives of whites and blacks were impeached to such a degree that bloodlines and surnames were shared. Like it or not, they were one people created in the cauldron of the Peculiar Institution. There was nothing uncommon about white babies nursing at the breasts of a black housekeeper. White politicians had a Negro (and most likely an Indian) hiding somewhere back in their family tree. If you went back to A.D. 700, *everyone on earth had a common ancestor; no two persons, regardless of* their race, could be less closely related than fiftieth cousins. Each man and woman on the planet today was a direct descendant of Jesus, Confucius, Gautama, Socrates, Tutankhamen, and Judas Iscariot. And, oh, interrelatedness went farther than even that. Each of the twenty thousand breaths we drew each day contained a quadrillion atoms breathed by the rest of humanity within the past week, and one's next breath brimmed with more than a million atoms that once swirled within the chests of Anaximander, Muhammad, Lao Tzu, Vivekananda, and the Aborigines of Australia. Given that ground of overlapping lives one could hope that once the artificial, legal barriers to integration were removed, the children of masters and slaves might recognize that Race was an illusion, all children were literally—genetically—their own, and embrace one another as members of a single tribe.

Yes, he knew the South. The North, of course, was another matter. Northern cities, he was ready to believe, were, as the Book of Genesis claimed, the products of Cain. Mercifully, they were behind him for another weekend.

And now the stewardess was moving his way, struggling with the editions it would take him over an hour to individually sign for her loved ones. Joints in his fingers would throb, he'd have to soak his hand later in a pan of hot water, as he often did after standing in receiving lines and pressing the flesh with thousands of admirers. And that was just all right. As Abu Sa'id, an Islamic scholar he admired, might put it, there was nothing inside the blue coat and skirt Stephanie was wearing except Allah.

5

We stayed on State Route 51 south from Carbondale, following a map Amy scrawled on the back of SCLC stationery as Smith did impersonations of the waitress Arlene and the old man in the Pit Stop. He was a remarkably talented mimic, I realized during the rest of the ride, and so scathingly funny in his interpretations that even while Amy and I laughed until tears cascaded down our cheeks, which helped me forget for a while my shame at the damage I'd done to the diner (every police car we passed made me squirm down in my seat), I was afraid to think of Smith applying his imitative skills on *me*. The possibility of seeing things as he did, from the oblique angle of alienation, fascinated and frightened me at the same time; he was so antithetical to King, yet in some ways I saw in Smith the distillation of the minister's message to a black student he met at Lycoming College in Pennsylvania, a young man so consumed by anger and hatred and dualism that all King could say was, "Son, the best thing you can do is try to understand yourself." Smith forced me to think on this, to turn it over and over, and inspect it from every side: My Self. Yet for all his similarities to King, his talk earlier about envy and divine rejection put me on edge— indeed, had briefly pushed me over it. My skinned knuckles were sore and I'd cut my left forearm when smashing bottles on the counter. In other words, I'd injured myself quite as much as I'd wasted the Pit Stop. And it was his—Chaym Smith's—doing. But slowly, as I saw him slip effortlessly into Arlene's physical eccentricities, I began to feel that, for all his exasperating qualities, perhaps he could stand in for King, and told him so.

"Sure, I can mark him," he said. "That's easy. Everybody's playing a role anyway, trying to act like what they're supposed to be, wearing at least one mask, probably more, and there's nothing underneath, Bishop. Just emptiness . . ."

The Chevelle coasted down a dusty road trenched between enormous trees that domed overhead, breaking sunlight into flecks of leaf-filtered brilliance that flickered on a road that wound past a dilapidated Methodist church and ended in front of a rough farmhouse. It seemed to spring up suddenly out of kudzu vines and broomsedge, a one-story structure erected on rocks: it floated above these huge stones like a raft, shadowed by a double-trunked oak tree in the yard. Paint on the front porch was peeling away in large strips like sunburned skin. The yard, wild with windblown weeds, was as uncultivated as a backfield full of burdocks and snakes. I cannot say I was relieved to arrive at this remote, rural destination. The heat was withering. Out there more than two miles from the highway, and possibly three to the nearest store, there were none of the distractions to rescue a man at night from the feelings and thoughts he least wanted to confront.

Or from the strangeness of Chaym Smith.

Skeptically he squinted at the dilapidated house. "Anybody living in this dump?"

"Not this summer." Amy's brow pleated. "And it's not a *dump*. Mama Pearl rents it out to kids over at the college. At her age she doesn't like to live so far from other people. It's furnished inside and she's never asked for more than what she needs to pay the taxes and keep her place upstate, but it's been empty since June. That church we passed up the road? Most of our family is buried in a cemetery there . . ."

Smith cut off the engine, and we unloaded the car, lugged boxes inside to dusty rooms with drop cloths covering the sparse, old-fashioned furnishings while Amy explained that her great-grandfather James, a preacher, framed each room and drove half the nails in the farmhouse as well as in the church just a quarter mile away.

Talking about her family was a natural, innocent enough thing to do, and she could not have known, nor I, how it would draw out even more of Smith's cynicism. Taking a deep breath, he said, "Is this gonna be a *long* story?"

I shot him a stare to shut him up as Amy opened stiff chintz curtains in the front room, flooding it with light. "Go on," I said. "You were saying something about your great-grandfather. What was he like?"

She was silent, looking around the room, remembering, and I was struck again by her beauty, the melic lift of her voice when Amy said she didn't know her great-grandfather all that well, but his daughter, Mama Pearl, often invoked her father as industrious and loving and quick to load his rifle if he caught the faintest trace of discrimination directed at either his kin or himself, though as a family the Griffiths seldom came into contact with whites, no more often than did, say, the Negroes who founded the town of Allensworth in California or other all-black hamlets at the turn of the century. Whites may not have liked them, but James—her grandmother told her—never asked to be liked, only respected. And that was a matter fully within their own control. They grew their own food before and after the crash that crippled the nation in '29. They operated a school for their children at the nearby church, one so successful in teaching metalwork that its graduates were considered the best smiths in the county and had work come rain or shine in the twenties.

Amy walked us through rooms of antique furniture—ladderbacked chairs, heavy oak tables, an old black walnut Jefferson bookstand fastened with mortise-and-tenon joinery—and for me it was like being gently led into the past, a distant, better time when black people were the moral fiber of a nation. She said that during her visits in the 1950s to Makanda nothing pleased her so much as how self-reliant her relatives and their neighbors seemed. There were inconveniences, of course. Water came from a well. Thirty paces from the back door was an outhouse she hated to visit in the middle of the night. But she loved seeing her kin making their own clothes and furniture and bartering with other black people in the area for the little they could not produce themselves. She remembered her great-grandfather, who, if he came across something he especially liked on his dinner plate, saved that portion of the meal for last; when he flipped through the newspaper and saw an item that interested him, he scanned everything else on that page first and held off satisfying his desire for that one particular news report until he'd made himself read everything around it. Throughout Jackson County her kin were known as the people black travelers should see if they were turned away from white hotels and needed a room for the night and a good meal the next morning. As might be expected, they had no tolerance for phoniness or pretense. They did not judge others by their possessions, dress, family pedigree, or how often they got their names in the newspaper. Family and friends came first. And they did not hesitate to share what little they had, whether it was food, labor, their home, or the skills each had developed in order to survive. She said they were known to hold on to a dollar until it hollered. (And James often discussed Negro entrepreneurs he admired, and urged his children to take as their example people like merchant Jean-Baptiste Du Sable, one of Chicago's earliest settlers, Madame Walker, Philadelphia's catering king Robert Bogle, and colored people who controlled America's service businesses before World War II, to say nothing of owning their own banks and insurance companies.) James's children, Mama Pearl and her two brothers, were never pampered. He insisted that from birth to age five his progeny be treated like princes and princesses, but after that they were to work like servants, even if what they did consisted in nothing more than fetching things for the other folks. (He suggested they sing as they worked to lighten the labor.) No, Amy said, he could not tolerate idleness, and it was not in his nature to ask anyone for anything.

As we traipsed through the old house, its floorboards creaking beneath our feet, Smith responded to Amy's family history with a contemptuous *pfft!* from his pursed lips, which puzzled me, because I almost felt that as Amy spoke I could hear her ancestors' day beginning with breakfast-table prayer, which did not exclude even the youngest children; they had to know chapter and verse before their twelfth birthday. There were no spirits in this household. In my mind, I saw James—a tall, dark-skinned, suspender-wearing black man—insisting that his two sons and daughter, Amy's grandmother, acquire as many skills as they had fingers on their hands, work for everything they received, and treat whatever possessions any family member had as carefully and conscientiously as if they belonged to someone else who one day might ask for their return. The family, he told them again and again, was far more than a group bonded by blood. More even than a collective that insured the survival of its members. More than anything else, according to the Griffith patriarch, it was the finest opportunity anyone would have for practicing selflessness, for giving to others day in, day out, and for this privilege, this chance to outgrow his own petty likes and dislikes, opinions and tastes, he gave abundant thanks. If they wanted to be happy, he counseled them, the first step was to make someone else happy. Through Amy's words I saw him demand that his children read after their chores were finished—what, he didn't care, but he wouldn't talk with them if two days had gone by and they'd not touched a book. (Smith was looking at his watch, frowning heavily; her story so displeased and rattled him that he entered one of the bedroom doorways at the same instant I did, and for a second we were stuck, shoulder to shoulder, our arms pinned at our sides, Chaplinesque, until I jerked free.) Eventually, she explained, the farm could not sustain itself. By the late 1950s, his sons left to find work elsewhere. Mama Pearl did the same, moving to Chicago, where she was steadily employed at Fanny's Restaurant in the suburb of Evanston, and possession of the property came to her when her mother died in 1963.

Now we were in the kitchen. Smith glowered darkly out the window, cracking his knuckles. I tried to ignore him. I said to Amy, "Your people lived like that?"

"Yes."

"I wish I'd known your great-grandfather." In the depths

of me I did. Partly I was envious, knowing so little of my own family's past before they migrated from the South to the city; and partly I hungered for the sense of history she had, the confidence and connectedness that came from a clear lineage stretching back a century. "He sounds like a wonderful man."

"He was." Amy laughed. "Mama Pearl told me he used to say over and over, 'Life is God's gift to you; what you do with it is your gift to Him'"

"Excuse *me*," growled Smith. "I need to shit."

Amy flinched, as though he'd pinched her. She pointed through the window to an outhouse about fifty feet from the back door. Smith seemed anxious to flee the farmhouse and had one foot out the door when she said, "Wait," reached into one of the boxes of SCLC materials we'd placed on the table, and brought out one of the Commitment Blanks distributed among volunteers. "I brought this along for you to sign."

I knew that form well, having signed one earlier in the year. On it were ten essential promises—like the tablets Moses hauled down from smoky Mount Sinai—the Movement asked of its followers. Seeing the form made me feel a little weak, insofar as I remembered the hundreds of times I'd failed to uphold these vows:

COMMANDMENTS FOR VOLUNTEERS

I HEREBY PLEDGE MYSELF—MY PERSON AND BODY—TO THE NONVIOLENT MOVEMENT. THEREFORE I WILL KEEP THE FOLLOWING COMMANDMENTS:

1. *Meditate* daily on the teachings and life of Jesus.
2. *Remember* always that the nonviolent movement seeks justice and reconciliation—not victory.

3. *Walk* and *Talk* in the manner of love, for God is
   love.
4. *Pray* daily to be used by God in order that all men
   might be free.
5. *Sacrifice* personal wishes in order that all men
   might be free.
6. *Observe* with both friend and foe the ordinary rules
   of courtesy.
7. *Seek* to perform regular service for others and for
   the world.
8. *Refrain* from the violence of fist, tongue, or heart.
9. *Strive* to be in good spiritual and bodily health.
10. *Follow* the directions of the movement and of the
    captain on a demonstration.

I sign this pledge, having seriously considered what I do
and with the determination and will to persevere.

NAME _____

(Please print neatly)

He tore it from her hand and tramped outside, his action
so rude—so brusque—that it startled Amy and angered me. I
followed him into the backyard, clamped my fingers on the
crook of his arm, and spun him round to face me.

"You want to tell me what's wrong?"

"That story she told," said Smith, "it's a fucking lie. Front
to back, it was *kitsch*. All narratives are lies, man, an illusion.
Don't you know that? As soon as you squeeze experience into
a sentence—or a story—it's suspect. A lot sweeter, or uglier,
than things actually were. Words are just webs. Memory is
mostly imagination. If you want to be free, you best go
beyond all that."

"To *what*?"

"That's what I'm trying to figure out. By the way"—he held up the Commitment Blank and grinned—"tell her thanks for this. I need something to wipe with."

I stood and watched him squeeze into the outhouse and shut the door. I picked up a handful of rocks and pegged them against the wall. Inside, Smith laughed. He reminded me I owed him for saving my skin in Chicago, and kept on talking through the door, railing against conformity and convention, all the while emptying his bowels loudly, with trumpeting flatulence and gurgling sounds and a stink so mephitic it made me choke, then fleeing back into the farmhouse, I found Amy looking through his bags.

Winged open in her hands was one of Smith's sketchbooks. She turned each page slowly, puzzling over verses he'd scrawled beneath a series of eight charcoal illustrations of a herdsman searching for his lost ox. Finding it. And leading it home, where—in the final panel—both hunter and hunted vanished in an empty circle. "Chaym is talented," she said as I stepped closer, looking over her shoulder, "but I can't see him helping the Movement. Look at these." She flipped through more pages, turning them carefully at the bottom edge, as if she were afraid the images might soil her fingers. But I was not seeing Smith's drawings. No. I saw only the softness of her skin, and before I knew full well what I was doing I encircled my arms round her waist and lowered my head to her shoulder in a kiss. Amy stiffened for an instant. Then I felt her relax, offering no resistance whatsoever to my embrace. She squeezed my arm gently, then stepped to one side and placed the sketchbook back on the kitchen table.

"That was sweet, Matthew, but please don't do it again."

"Why not?"

"I know you're attracted to me," she said. "I *know* that. And I'm flattered. I really am. It's just that I'm not right for you. Or you for me. Your sign is water—didn't you say that once? Mine is earth. Together, all we'd make is *mud*." She tried to laugh, to get me to laugh, as one might a child who has knocked over his water glass at the table and needs to be chastised but not crushed for his blindness. His blunder. She was not angry, only disappointed, I thought, and was doing her best to be gracious—to salvage the situation for me and herself—after the minor mess I'd created. And it was strange, I realized, how at that moment my emotions were a pastiche of pain and wonder at her civilized composure, her ability to absorb the discomfort and disorientation my desire caused her—as if she were stepping over a puddle—and at the same time transform it into something like sympathy for me, for how confused and aching I felt right then—like someone who'd fallen off a ladder, say, or stepped on a rake. Yes, that was how I felt. Gently she placed her hand on my arm, and in a voice as full of candor as it was of Galilean compassion, said, "I'm fond of you, really I am, but I'm not the right person for you." Once again she smiled, as one might when a child is being unreasonable. "Someday, if you do well, you'll find someone right for you. I need somebody a little more like the men I knew when I was growing up. Or like Dr. King. Oh, God, I hope I haven't hurt you."

Actually I couldn't say; I'd never been shot down with such finesse before. Nor had I ever felt so impoverished by desire. Just then, her words were more than I could bear.

"We can still be friends?"

I couldn't look at her, but I said, "Sure." My eyes began to burn and steam, blurring the buckled, floral-print linoleum floor as she pushed up on her toes, pressing her lips against my cheek in a chaste kiss. "I suppose we should get back to unpacking, eh?"

"You go ahead, I'll get Chaym."

More than anything else, I needed to be away from the

farmhouse. And her. It was dark now. My feet carried me east, from the kitchen to an open field. Looking back at the lighted rear window of the old, warm house with its family heirlooms and positivist history as it grew smaller, I felt better being outside, stepping through humus, round moss-covered stones green as kelp, past the well where the water tasted faintly of minerals, skinks, and salamanders. The brisk walk left me panting a little, perspiring as if a spigot somewhere in my pores had switched on, pouring out toxins in a tamasic flush of sweat that soaked my shirt. Yes, it still hurt. I'd always known I was hardly the model for Paul's Epistle in Corinthians 13, but to be rebuffed because I fell so short of the minister's example was confounding. Who could measure up to *that*? Yet—and yet—in her refusal I also felt relief, as if the weight of want had lifted. I sat down in weeds high as my waist, the night closing round me like two cupped hands. Wondering less about the woman I'd desired than the mystery of my desire itself, how it had made me experience myself as *lack* and her as fulfillment, all of which were false, mere fictions of my imagination. Just beyond there were woods that looked vaporous and incorporeal in the moonlight; and I felt just as vaporous and incorporeal, as if maybe I might vanish in the enveloping, prehuman world around me. Leaves on the nearest trees trembled with tiny globes of moisture clear as glass. And then, as my eyes began to adjust, I saw numinal light haloing the head of a figure—it was Smith—kneeling amidst the trees.

His eyes were seeled, his breath flowed easily, lifting his chest at half-minute intervals and flaring the flanges of his nostrils faintly with each inhalation. His exterior was still as a figure frozen in ice. Yet inside, I knew from his notebooks, he was in motion, traversing 350 passages he'd memorized from numerous spiritual traditions, allowing the words to slip through his mind like pearls on a necklace. The passages—called *gatha* in Buddhist monasteries—ranged from Avaita Vedanta to Thomas à Kempis, from Seng Ts'an to the devotional poetry of Saint Teresa of Avila, from the Qur'an to Egyptian hymns, from a phrase in John 14:10 to the Dhammapada; they were tools—according to jottings he'd made—selected to free him from contingency and the conditioning of others. When he focused on a *gatha,* the *gatha* was his mind for that moment, identical with it, knower and known inseparable as water and wave. He was utterly unaware of me, and his practicing the Presence, reviewing these passages like a Muslim *hafiz,* was so private and intimate an exercise that I felt like a voyeur and was about to pull myself away, back toward the farmhouse, when I saw tears sliding down his cheekbones to his chin.

Then his eyes were open, and he asked softly, "You like what you see, Bishop?" He wiped his cheeks with the back of his hand. "Yeah, I cry sometimes. Can't help myself. When I sit, it just comes out. I can't keep it down. At the *zendo,* I wasn't the only one who cried when doing *zazen.*"

I stepped closer and sat down as he stretched out his legs from the kneeling position, massaging them vigorously to get blood moving again. "Where was that?"

"Kyoto," he said. "Two years after my discharge I was there, tossing down sake, and the fellah I was drinking with told me 'bout a Zen temple way out in the forest that accepted foreigners. 'Bout that time I was a mess, man. Drank like a fish. Hurt inside every damned day. I wanted to kill myself. Kept my service revolver right beside my pillow, just in case I worked up the courage to stick the barrel in my mouth and paint the wall behind me with brains. I went to the temple 'cause I was sick and tired of the world. I wanted a refuge, someplace where I could heal myself. I figured it was either the *zendo* or I was dead." Smith kept on massaging his right leg as he talked, working his way methodically from his hip downward.

"When I got there, I kneeled in front of the entrance, on the steps, and kept my head bowed until I heard the straw sandals of one of the priests coming toward me. I begged him to let me train. Naturally, he refused my request, like he was supposed to do, and then he went away. That's the script. So I sat there all day—like I was supposed to do—on my knees, my head bowed, keeping that posture and waiting. Night came, but I still didn't move. On the second day it rained. I was soaked to the skin. I damned near caught pneumonia on the second evening. But sometime during the third day the priest came back and gave me permission to enter the temple temporarily. See, he was playing a role thousands of years old—same as I was playing mine. He had me wash my feet, gave me a pair of tatami sandals, put me in a special little room called *tankaryo,* shut the sliding paper door, and went away again, this time for five days. For five days, I didn't see nobody. They didn't bring me food. Or water. I waited, kneeling just like you seen me doing, my eyes shut, hands on my lap, palms up with my thumbs kissing my forefingers, meditating for a hundred twenty hours nonstop to prove to the priest that I could do it. I say five days, but when you're in *zazen* that long, there is no time. That's another illusion, Bishop. In God, or the Void—or whatever you wanna call it—past, present, and future are all rolled up in *now.* And the hardest thing a man can do, especially a colored man whose ass has been kicked in every corner of the world, is live completely in *now.* But I did. And the priest came back. He led me down a hallway with wooden floors polished so brightly by hand that they almost gleamed, then he stopped in front of a bulletin board listing the names of the monks and laymen presently training at the temple. Mine was the last, the newest one there. I tell you, buddy, when I seen that I broke down and cried like a goddamn baby. I was home. You get it? After centuries of slavery and segregation and being shat on by everybody on earth, I was *home*."

I did get it, and in his voice I saw the beautiful vision of a tile-roofed, forest temple encircled by trees, the grounds spotless, the gardens well tended, and here and there were statues of guardian kings. Smith began slowly massaging his left leg as he'd done his right, working from hip to heel.

"I was a good novice, I want you to know that. Every day I was up at three-thirty A.M. when the priest struck the sounding board. When I washed up I didn't waste a drop of water. I brushed my teeth using only one finger and a li'l bit of salt, and I was the first in the Hondo—the Buddha hall—for the morning recitation of sutras. After that, when we ate, I didn't drop nary a grain of rice from my eating bowl. I shaved my head every five days. Kept my robes mended. With the others, I walked single file from the temple into town, reciting sutras and collecting donations in a cloth bag suspended from a strap around my neck. Always I blessed those who gave, singing a brief sutra that all sentient beings may achieve enlightenment and liberation. But for that year I trained, I never touched money. Or thought 'bout women. Or drink. The world that hurt me so bad didn't exist no more, and I was happy. Hell, I wasn't even aware of an *I*. After our rounds we came back and did *samu*—monastic labor. Chopping firewood. Maintaining the gardens. And all this we did in silence, Bishop. Each daily task was *zazen*. Was holy. No matter how humble the work, it was all spiritual practice."

Smith had finished stretching. He scooted back from the spot where he'd been sitting and rested his back against a tree.

"What I'm saying is that my practice was correct. So good the Roshi promoted me to kitchen chef or *tenzo*. That's an honor, right? It means I'd been diligent. He put me in charge of preparing food to sustain the *Sangha*, and I was 'bout the only one the Old Man, the Roshi, didn't whack with his bamboo stick when time came for him to interview me 'bout my *koan*.

"It was great," Smith said. Then, sourly, "For a year."

"What happened? Why'd you leave?"

"Didn't want to." He laughed. "I felt like I was in Shangri-la. I coulda stayed there forever. But one year to the very day I started, one of the priests said the Roshi wanted to see me. I was in the kitchen, making a sauce to go with wheat-paste noodles. Lemme tell you, it was *good*. Li'l sea tangle, sesame seeds, ginger, chopped green onions, and grated radishes. I washed my hands, then hurried to the Roshi's room. I struck the *umpan*, the gong, to let him know I'd arrived, then entered when he called. I knelt before him, never lifting my eyes, but I wondered fiercely why he wanted to see me. Had I done wrong? No, he told me. My practice was perfect. The other monks respected me. But (he said) I was a *gaijin*. A foreigner. Only a Japanese could experience true enlightenment. That's what he said. He didn't want me to waste my time. He was being compassionate—see?—or thought he was. I left that night, Bishop. If anything, my year in the temple taught me what Gautama figured out when he broke away from the holy men: if you want liberation, to be free, you got to get there on your own. All the texts and teachers are just tools. If you want to be free, you're *supposed* to outgrow them."

"I'm sorry," I said.

"Don't feel sorry. There's no place anywhere for me. I seen that a long time ago. Wherever I go, I'm a nigger. Oh, and I been to mother Africa. Over there, where people looked like me, I didn't fit either. I don't belong to a tribe. To them I was an American, a black one, and that meant I didn't belong anywhere." He patted his pants and shirt, searching for his cigarettes. Having found the pack in his breast pocket, Smith lit one with a Zippo lighter, and blew a smoke ring my way. Then quietly he asked, "What about you? Do you feel at home—*really* at home—anywhere?"

"No." I thought of my blundering pass earlier in the farmhouse. "I don't. Ever . . ."

"Then you're damned too," Smith said. "You got the mark. That's what I seen on you. Outcasts know each other. The blessed know us too, and keep their distance, and I can't say I blame 'em. We scare 'em. We make 'em uncomfortable. We're the unwanted, the ones always passed over. Until the day we die, we're drifters. Won't no place feel right for long. And that's okay. I accept that. Hell, I embrace it. My spirit don't ever have to be still. It don't need to sleep. Fuck that. The only thing is, I don't want to be forgotten. Not by the goddamn sheep. Or God. I want to *do* something to make Him remember this nigger—*me*—for eternity.

Then Smith was quiet for a while, staring past me toward the lights of the farmhouse, and something in me quieted as well. He was a man without a home. Without a race. I pitied him and myself, for what he'd said about knowing no place on earth where he could find peace and security was something I'd often felt and feared, and perhaps that was even why I wanted—or believed I wanted—Amy. Now I feared it less, and for the first time since Chaym Smith surfaced during the Chicago riots, I understood the labyrinthal depths of his (our) suffering. Or did I? Hadn't he said all stories were lies? What, then, was I to make of the one he'd just told me? It had seduced me, but as always I didn't exactly know where truth ended and make-believe began with him.

"What will you do?" I asked. "Doc told us to help you—"

"Help me, then." He got to his feet, brushing grass off the seat of his britches. "Best thing you and the girl can do is teach me what I don't know about Dr. King." His smile gleamed in the moonlight, followed by that maddening, ticlike wink. "Do that, and I'll take care of everything else."

6

At the SCLC part of my job description was recording the
Revolution, preserving its secrets for posterity—particularly
what took place in the interstices. Naturally, this is where
the stories of all doubles occur. In a spiral notebook, one I
kept from my college days, I made entries on Chaym Smith's
progress, having no idea at the time that just possibly I was
composing a gospel. I—even I—was startled to discover how
much he'd already absorbed about King since 1954, as a man
might meticulously study his rival, or an object of love, or—
in his case—someone he loved and envied simultaneously.
He was determined to *possess* the mystery of the minister's
power and popularity, to make it his own. In the days following our arrival at the Nest, one flowing into the next in a
round-the-clock ribbon of dress rehearsals for the role Smith
was set on playing, we three were subtly transformed, Amy

no less than I as we looked to impress the matrix of the minister onto our charge.

Of course, he began with the Bible, rereading his heavily underlined New Testament in a marathon review that began Friday late and lasted well into the following Monday. His capacity for sustained, one-pointed concentration was uncanny, a skill—that of *dharana*—he'd acquired during his year at the temple in Kyoto. He highlighted in red every statement by Jesus, who most certainly was known as "Joshua" in his own time and possibly was a member of the Essenes, a Jewish monastic order influenced by Hinduism. Around the farmhouse Smith had Amy pin photographs of everyone important in King's life and sheets of paper containing the scriptural citations most often encountered in his sermons. These he committed to memory, sometimes through rote repetition, sometimes through mnemonic devices that allowed him to absorb whole speeches, provided he could call up the pictorial "pegs" on which key phrases and ideas had been placed. Soon enough it became clear that as Smith immersed himself in the first thirty-seven years of King's journey, he was entering a portal that, far from stopping at the borders of the black world or the Baptist faith, exploded outward into what King himself once called, in a phrase far more revealing of himself than he knew, the "inescapable network of mutuality."

He sent me to the state college over in Carbondale, where I photocopied the available sermons by preachers who'd influenced King's oratorical style. This took a full day, and led to the startling (for me) and exhilarating (for Smith) discovery that many of the minister's most famous speeches were tissues of pirated material from nearly three dozen theologians and popular (white) American preachers from the '40s and '50s, their ideas and idioms, voices and vocabularies, so blended with his own blistering denunciations of bigotry that, once I brought these documents back to the Nest, we found it impossible to demarcate where the minds (and the archaeology of that most ancient of objects, the self) of Harry Emerson Fosdick, C. L. Franklin, and Robert McCracken ended and King's properly commenced. In his sermons he was, in essence, not one man but an integrated Crowd, containing here a smidgen of Walter Rauschenbusch, there a bit of Gerald Kennedy, and everywhere the imposing influence of his father. In effect, the minister riffed (not unlike Louis Armstrong or Duke Ellington) on the entire, two-millennia-old history of Christendom, blending its best and making that his own in a stunningly Yankee amalgam.

Smith found this discovery of some of King's sources, his borrowings, gratifying. Gleefully so. "You know, I always figured he couldn't be as smart as he seems," Smith said, yet I doubted he believed that. He was looking for faults, anything to reduce the minister's stature and give himself room to breathe. But I wondered, as we examined King's intellectual genesis and his Elizabethan borrowings, if the self we constructed was anything more than a fragile composite of other selves we'd encountered—a kind of epistemological salad—indebted to all spoken languages, all evolutionary forms, all lives that preceded our own, so that, when we spoke, it could be said, in the final analysis, subjectivity vanished and the world sang in every sentence we uttered. (And thus narrative was not a lie.) Added to that, and perhaps strangest of all, I noticed that as Smith pored over King's speeches he at first resisted statements that contradicted his own experience of things—for example, the minister saying, "It is quite easy for me to think of the universe as basically friendly mainly because of my uplifting heredity and environmental circumstances." In learning, there was an inescapable moment of alienation and displacement, a plunge into uncertainty and insecurity in the new, the *other*; but then, miraculously, as he relaxed from resisting the revolution possible with each new perception, that interval of disorientation passed, and he found that no matter how far his mind had traveled, or how alien the data of knowledge might have seemed at first, he had in the end through these studies encountered only a dimension of himself.

After I worked with Smith all morning and afternoon on the broad themes and tropes in the minister's speeches, and the four levels of meaning in the Bible (literal, allegorical, tropological, and anagogic), and helped him design for himself a daily program of *lectio divina*, stretching the envelope of his mind and imagination, he enlisted Amy to work on his body. He knew, of course, exactly what he wanted from us. At the temple, Smith said, he'd learned to read Sanskrit in three days of study and chanting sutras. He asked Amy, who'd been a drama student, to help him with exercises to control the vocal centers—the abdomen, chest, lower and upper throat, and sinus cavity. He had me give him a close-to-the-skull haircut.

Then he proceeded to study, for fifty-minute intervals (as monks do with mandalas), and with all his senses imaginatively put into play, color photographs of King's birth home (sold to Rev. Williams in 1909 for the price of $3,500) at 501 Auburn Avenue N.E. in Atlanta. With these pictures spread out before him on the farmhouse floor, he imaginatively climbed the four steps to the door and worked to *feel* everything in the images, bringing forth an emotional association for the umbrella box, high-backed chair, and table with a bouquet of flowers in the entryway; *feel* his way past the sliding doors to the piano with its low bench, which had one wobbly leg, the fireplace, the rocker, and different games— Old Maid and Monopoly—the King children played beside the old-fashioned radio in the parlor; *feel* himself walking the hardwood floors from the parlor to the tiny first-floor bathroom where Martin as a boy hid from his father's switch and to avoid the unmanly chore of doing the dishes (he preferred to haul coal for the furnace to the cramped, low-ceilinged basement); he moved on to the kitchen with its Hossier cabinets and icebox containing a frozen block weighing ten pounds. From the kitchen window he worked to see the vacant lot the King children often played in and where once a year the circus, featuring clowns and acrobats and sweet cones of colored ice, threw up its tents. He ascended to the second floor, where he could view from the stairhead, one hand resting on the smooth railing, the window Martin used to leap from to impress girls passing by, and at age twelve hurled himself from with suicidal intent after hearing of "Mama" Jennie Williams's fatal heart attack in 1941 when *he* had sneaked away to sin by going to the circus. He let his gaze travel to the guestroom (far left) set aside by King Senior for the endless stream of visiting ministers who stayed at their home; then on to his grandmother's bedroom (there Martin was born), and next to that the boy's playroom, where Tinkertoys, Lincoln Logs, coloring books, and Chinese checkers were scattered along the floor, and to feel too the height of the second-floor ceiling which Daddy King, who was only five-six, touched with his fingertips when he learned of Martin's birth and literally jumped for joy. (Martin, we informed Smith, was originally named Michael King Jr. after his father, who was also christened Michael and then later, like his son, replaced that name with Martin.) We could see that this exercise was excruciating for Chaym Smith. He'd lived in an orphanage. On the streets. Each detail in the photos reinforced for him the staggering inequities of personal fortune. Little wonder that King leaned more toward optimism than pessimism about human nature. Toward the end of this session, as Smith came back downstairs and out to the front porch, giving himself a clear image of the German store down the street, owned by the father of Martin's two best friends, and just across the street, over the neatly trimmed shrubs in the Kings' yard, the shotgun shacks and alley apartments housing the black poor only fifty feet from Daddy King's front door—at the end, Smith was shaken. He said, "I woulda given anything for a loving, decent childhood like that. Parents like that." He peered up to me, but his eyes were still filled with all he'd seen. "Bishop, it ain't right not having anybody who cared . . ."

Amy thought it best to put the photos away.

That night he slept longer than usual, his dreams peopled with King family principals. Loving folk such as Smith himself had never known. We did not wake him. He stumbled from his bedroom a little before noon, still bitter, but said, "What're y'all staring at me for? Let's get to work." In Chicago, King had given us several articles of his clothing: pointed black shoes, a shirt from Zimmerman's in Atlanta, black shin-high nylon socks, a brown passport holder bearing the inscription CITY OF LONDON, HOUSE OF PARLIAMENT, and Ruskin's book *Unto This Last*. These I gave to Smith. The clothing was a near-perfect fit. After a light lunch, he turned to copying lines from one of King's recorded speeches, "A Knock at Midnight," isolating the metaphoric logic behind the comparisons King drew, some of which Smith found severely wanting in poetic value ("the cataract of sin," "the virus of pride"); he sneered, "I can do better than that," then plunged on to scan passages ("Nót ónly is ít mídnight in mán's colléctive lífe bút it's mídnight ín his individual life, ít's mídnight in the psychólógical ordér . . .") so his emphasis would vary as little as possible from the original.

To his credit and our incredulity, he absorbed the information we fed him like a sponge. But then again, the task was not as daunting as it might seem, given his long, painful twelve-year obsession with the nation's most prominent preacher, and his own unusual gifts. Little by little, he learned that if there was a single philosophical law to the minister's life, an essence, it was embodied in three profound ideals. First, the deeper meaning of nonviolence, not merely as a strategy for protest, but as a Way, a daily praxis men must strive to translate into each and every one of their deeds. This Smith understood and compared to the Sanskrit word *ahimsa,* from *himsa* ("to injure") and *a* ("no" or "not"), so that in its fullness King's moral stance implied noninjury to everything that exists. Second, *agape,* the ability to love something not for what it presently was (which might be quite unlovable, like George Wallace) but for what it could be, a teleological love that recognized everything as process, not product, and saw beneath the surface to a thing's potentiality. And last, the fact of integration as the life's blood of Being itself. As I explained this to Smith, it struck me that these were not separate ideals at all, only different sides of a single meditation nearly as old as humanity, a meditation that could be lapped and folded in as few as three words:

Others *first.*

Always.

That was the vision; everything else was mere detail. (Though the Devil, as always, was in the details.)

Nights, when he slept, crashing into unconsciousness, Smith placed close by his mattress a tape recorder that all night long softly played Donizetti's *Lucia di Lammermoor,* "Moonlight" Sonata, Mahalia Jackson, and compositions by Harry T. Burleigh. Awakening the next day at 5 A.M., his eyes puffy, he put aside his razor, substituting for it the distinctly black ritual of shaving with the smelly depilatory powder ("Magic") used by the minister and, if truth be told, millions of black men with sensitive skin. It lit up the farmhouse with a smell like sulfur or eggs gone south after he mixed it with cold water, spread it on his face with a spatula, let it harden for five minutes, then scraped it off. But it wasn't enough for Smith to shave like King; he elected to eat as he did too, having Amy fix meals of the minister's favorite dishes—turnip greens, bacon drippings, and cornbread (food, King once confessed, was his greatest sin). I helped in the kitchen, reading to Amy from Mama Pearl's recipes, and shared with her the chore of washing (me) and drying (Amy) her family's plates, silverware, and pots after dinner. But no, I did not approach her again with my affections. I was even careful, when handing her a plate for drying, to keep two feet of distance between us, and I was at pains not to bump into her or touch her without her permission, or look at her for too long, or do *any*thing that would make her uncomfortable or remember how clumsily I'd cast my heart at her feet only to have her step around it like roadkill.

No doubt my behavior baffled her (which was nothing new). Like so many in the Movement, Amy was strong, serious, sure of herself and what things meant in the world. She was an Abelite, lost to ambiguity. I cannot lie; I loved her still. I'd believed that as Aquinas, that intractable Aristotelian, put it, a pious woman might lead a man to the Lord. Saint John of the Cross said it just as well, *amado con amada*. She might be his salvation, if he wedded his will to hers. (Clearly, this worked for King's father.) But I knew my love would never be returned. This asymmetry was not entirely unsatisfying. Because of Smith, I began to accept the sad inevitability of myself. With not being able to take sides (when one's choices were miserable). With the mark of loneliness, ipseity, Socratic doubts, interiority, and always having an afterthought. I felt at ease with (and less apologetic for) my bookishness, my inclination toward irony, and my sense that the world as it was, was unacceptable; I'd settled on the fact that perhaps I lived best as a witness who withdrew and gained distance in order to become truly engaged. Still, I recognized something I loved in the community of the certain, the blessed, but thanks to Smith I hankered for it a little less than before and knew that whatever liberation I might look forward to was in my hands alone.

And there is also this to say:

I began to fear we were being watched. Although I said nothing to the others, late some nights a plain green Plymouth rolled up the road toward the farmhouse. Its headlights were off. The driver sat for long minutes, and I saw smoke spiraling up through one side window. We were miles from town; I wondered: Who would come this far? Whenever I rose from bed and ran barefoot to the road, the Plymouth's engine started, and the car was gone before I got there, nothing remaining of its presence except tire marks and black dottle from someone's pipe.

As I said, I did not want to frighten the others. Instead, I asked Smith to walk with me, just to get him away from his regimen of reading, to Giant City State Park, through the enclosure known as the Stone Fort, which once served as a site for Indian ceremonial purposes at the top of an eighty-foot stone cliff. As we walked I tried to convey capsule descriptions of existentialist theologians germane to the minister's intellectual genesis, and what little I'd gleaned from a hasty perusal of Edgar Brightman. Of Personalism there was precious little to say. Had King not written about its value to him in reinforcing his belief in a loving, divine Father on high when he was in college (in contrast to Paul Tillich's monistic, impersonal God as the "Ground of Being"), Personalism as a philosophy would be as dead as Neoplatonism. None of the abstract portraits of the Lord offered by Tillich, Plotinus, Spinoza, or Eastern mystics could satisfy a Baptist preacher's boy. Thus the Boston Personalists, and Crozer professor L. Harold DeWolf's conception of a self-limited, temporal Father who bore man's face and flaws, hopes and values, impacted on King's vision more than any other; if Martin imagined the Lord, the odds were good that He looked (and behaved) more than a little like Daddy King. For DeWolf, God was immersed in creation, His power willingly curtailed by human freedom. He was not a prescient deity. His holiness was entangled in the bloody advance of history. Future events unfolding in this intentionally less than best of all possible worlds might take Him by surprise. He did not will suffering. Evil on earth was beyond his control, but in the Father's contract with His children, evil was an opportunity for spiritual growth and triumph. The Devil could not prevail, for as man struggled from innocence through sin to redemption he waged a war on His behalf to realize history's goal of the Heavenly City, the kingdom. King, I explained, accepted some restrictions on God's power, but could not—would not—believe for a second that He lacked absolute control of events predestined to lead to social liberation and the beloved community.

On our way back to the Nest, tramping along quietly at my side with his hands folded across his midsection (a carry-over from his temple training, the position known as *shashu*, "forked hands"), his brow furrowed, Smith was brooding. Out of the corner of my eye, I checked him, uneasy by how now he seemed more like the minister than before. "I'm starting to see something," he said. "Martin don't hold back nothing for himself." We tramped on, his silence freighted as he wrestled with his thoughts. "He's about total surrender, giving it all to God. I been trying to get a handle on him, but sometimes it's like he ain't there. Like he's an instrument, not the music itself—a conduit for something else that's always just outta my reach."

"Do you have faith?" I asked.

"What?"

"I said, do you have faith, Chaym?"

"Naw." His brow tightened. "None. How *could* I? If you're saying that's why I've got the shell but not the substance, fuck you, Bishop. There's nothing *but* shell, far as I can see. And I'm ready now. You understand? I can do anything *he* does. Just watch me—and I'll fucking do it better."

The call from Doc came on August 4.

Routinely, I'd driven into Carbondale to phone the Lawndale flat, report on Smith's progress, and keep abreast of the campaign in Chicago. The minister, whose voice was flat and tired, as if he could barely stay awake, asked if we could return for the Marquette march. In the background I heard arguing, voices I could not identify, but the heart of this contentious discussion seemed to center on the escalating backlash against King's lieutenants, some of them having picketed real estate agencies in the Belmont-Cragin area, and for their trouble saw their parked cars set on fire. SCLC and CCCO workers were at the end of their patience. When King was away, Andrew Young and Al Raby led fifteen hundred demonstrators (they were still falling far short of the turnout they needed) into an Irish-Lithuanian neighborhood near Marquette Park on July 30. The marchers were heckled by residents waving Confederate flags and homemade signs reading NIGGER, HOW YOU WISH YOU WERE WHITE and SEGREGATION IS GOD'S PLAN. Their parked cars were pushed into a lagoon. Predictably, the Chicago police were no help whatsoever. Their cousins and kin lived in these all-white enclaves; after pushing irate white residents into wagons with CENTRAL DETENTION SERVICE labeled on their rear doors they drove them a few blocks away and set them free. Those neighborhoods were explosive, someone in the rundown flat told

King. A powder keg waiting to be lit. The minister excused himself, asking me to hold, and I heard him say he agreed the moment was right for confrontation.

Waiting in a phone booth at a rural filling station six hours away from the city, I realized that our weeks downstate, away from newspapers and televisions, had thrown me out of step with the breathless pace of King's northern campaign. Chicago was still reeling from the riots. The monolith of de facto segregation had barely budged an inch. Blacks were squeezed into ten percent of the city's area, with only four percent living in the suburbs, where homes ran as high as $15,000. The CCCO, which gave priority to changing inferior education over economic boycotts, was battling to oust despised emblems of segregation in the schools like superintendent Benjamin C. Willis and a high school principal named Miss Chuchut. Yet despite setbacks by Democratic precinct ward-organizers who threatened the poor with loss of their welfare payments if they voted or protested, a degree of progress had been made. Using as their model the tactics of Philadelphia's Rev. Leon Sullivan, King's forces created a local chapter of Operation Breadbasket and designated as its director a University of Chicago theology student named Jesse Jackson in a move that ruffled the feathers of more than a few older activists, but the bold young minister did bring home the bacon when a boycott led to better employment for blacks with the Country Delight Dairy chain.

Nevertheless, too little had changed in a campaign that noisily blew into town promising to bring down the walls of economic racism once and for all. Real estate agencies were making a killing off white flight from neighborhoods that in just months turned completely black. Gun sales soared in Slavic districts, and I wondered, as the minister must have wondered, if it was possible to end social evil through actions that did not themselves engender a greater, more devastating evil. Back in 1954, the newspapers had labeled the Montgomery Improvement Association's nonviolent bus boycott "Gandhian." The Movement picked up the phrase later, and King was fond of saying Jesus provided the message, Gandhi the method for their social mission. But this was not entirely true. Nor, strictly speaking, faithful to Gandhi, who claimed *his* greatest ambition was "To make myself zero." When asked for the secret of his life, the mahatma replied, *Tena tyaktena bhunjithah* ("Renounce and enjoy"). Howard University activists appropriated the approach of nonviolent civil disobedience in the 1940s, when King was still in college. His version derived from theirs, the Howard leaders who took the body but not necessarily the soul of the mahatma's method, the surface but not the deepest impulse to renounce materialism and egotism in all their manifestations. Far from being anchored in the dualism of the Christian book, Gandhi's methods drew from the Bhagavad Gita, which taught him, he insisted, that "those who desire salvation should act like the trustee who, though having control over great possessions, regards not an iota of them as his own." Selfless, humble, detached, living without privacy so that his life was perfectly transparent, seeking no personal gain or profit, indefatigable, Gandhi could meet any social conflict head-on for those he loved, and his intention was never to humiliate or beat down his opponent. *How to end evil without engendering error or evil.* The question had apparently slowed down Howard's activists and the SCLC and the CCCO not at all.

Back on the phone, asking the others in the room to hold the noise down, the minister said, "You can be here then? We need everyone now to help . . ."

"Yes, sir," I said. "We'll be there by morning."

Although uneventful, the ride north took longer by two hours because the Chevelle blew a fan belt outside Centralia, and I had to hike to a service station, buy a replacement, then walk back to the car. Smith rode in back with Amy, wearing one of the minister's dark blue suits, his patterned tie, and clockface cufflinks. From head to toe he was as immaculate as the minister himself when he attended Morehouse and was affectionately known as Tweed. As spit-shined as King felt he had to be at Crozer to bury the stereotype of the Negro as slovenly. Just hours earlier, Amy'd packed his hair with Murray's Pomade so the waves stood out in neat little rows; she'd creamed his face with Nadinola to clear up a few of his pimples, and he'd splashed on some of the minister's favorite aftershave lotion, Aramis. On the whole, Smith looked uncomfortable in a suit, with a starched white collar squeezing his throat. And perhaps he was nervous, afraid he would fail at this job he'd petitioned for just as he'd failed at everything else. (And no, we could not keep Smith from strapping on his .357 Magnum, despite my telling him that King, while he did not oppose self-defense, felt edgy if anyone around him wore firearms because years before one of his bodyguards in the South had nearly shot a paperboy.) Amy kept inspecting him, pinching lint off his jacket and from his hair, wetting her handkerchief and rubbing at spots of shaving powder still on his jaw. Surely working so closely with him had been as much a trial for her as it was for me. At the Nest, I noticed that whenever Smith spoke disparagingly about other races—Jews, Chinese, or whites—Amy's eyes glazed over and grew quiet; they became distant, wall-like, and a sadness fell around her like a scrim. It was not in her nature to make sweeping remarks about any race or group. By the time we returned to the city, Smith, knowing he needed our help, and not wishing to displease her, had shed generalizations of that kind, at least when around Amy.

Come eight o'clock we were on Edens Expressway. I stopped by a service station, where I called Doc again. He did not want a double standing in during the march. No, that duty was too important to relegate to others. He only wanted us nearby. King was optimistic, upbeat. But when the hour of the demonstration arrived, as the temperature climbed to the eighties and I pulled in behind other vehicles entering Gage Park, I felt his decision to keep us on the sidelines was a tactical error.

Smith, fingering a carbuncle on his forehead, saw the crowd first and muttered, "Damn! This ain't no way to wage a fuckin' war!" Six hundred Negroes and their white supporters from all walks of life, including the clergy, were gathered on the grass, supported by twelve hundred policemen. Over a thousand angry residents waited, itching for trouble, hooting racial insults and waving flags bearing the Nazi swastika and handwritten signs proclaiming THE ONLY WAY TO END NEGROES IS EXTERMINATION. Tension in the air was thick enough to make me short-winded. The mood was carnival-like—but this circus was from Gehenna, with the sort of gaiety you'd expect from townfolk turning out for the year's biggest lynching, eagerly awaiting more excitement than they could see that summer at a hundred Riverviews. I stepped out of the Chevelle for a moment, carrying a two-way radio to keep in contact with Amy, sweat streaming inside my clothes, down my back, and into my shoes. I prayed that King would come to his senses, change his mind, and stay in the white compact car ahead of us. If he'd ever needed conclusive evidence that the SCLC was out of its element, the swelling mob of young, working-class, Nordic-looking white males in sweaty T-shirts, or with their shirts tied around their throats, straining against the police to get their hands on the marchers—he damned well had *that* proof now. Down South, they were accustomed to crowds of maybe fifty or seventy. Violent whites were few, a minority of rabble-rousers easily rousted by federal troops. But here? Oh, here they came pouring from their homes in waves, the young and the old, healthy and infirm, Polish, Germans, and Italians who fought among themselves constantly but today were bonded by blood against a common foe determined, they believed, to take away their precious homes. The boys had greasy, slicked-back hair and packs of cigarettes rolled up in their T-shirt sleeves at shoulder level like refugees from movies starring Marlon Brando and Sal Mineo. One, with his cap turned backward, could have been Leo Gorcey. Others wore dark sunglasses. Cowboy hats. Handkerchiefs were wrapped as headbands across their brows. Watching them as they poured into the park, some riding on the shoulders of others in order to see and shouting, *We want King!*, I realized they had come far better prepared than Doc's people. Cherry bombs, difficult to distinguish from gunfire, exploded around the Chevelle and King's car as we inched forward into a sea of urban thugs. Rotten eggs splattered the Chevelle's windshield, coating it so I couldn't see and started swearing when my wipers failed to work. I turned the car over to Amy and scrambled out into the crowd, hoping to get closer to the minister's car. On my left, good white Catholics spit in the faces of priests and nuns committed to civil rights. My heart was hammering. Now I knew why Smith had said we— Negroes—were despised worldwide, for we had done nothing to this crowd. Nothing to earn such revulsion and violence. In fact, there was something biblical, mythic, and ritualistic in their hatred of their darker brothers, something in the blood, as if to found and sustain a city, a sacrificial slaughter must take place. Beer-bellied white men, cigars tucked in the corners of their mouths, screamed for King's appearance and pounded on the park's grass with baseball bats. Others chanted white power slogans, calling the black marchers (who carried signs that read HOW LONG? and OPEN UP CHICAGO!) monkeys. They shouted, "Where's Martin Luther Coon!" and "Kill the nigger-lovers!" at cops who to their astonishment found themselves faced off (Matthew 10:34–39) against their own cousins, sisters, and in-laws.

Into this chaos stepped King.

He emerged from his car into a shower of spit, rocks, beer bottles, and firecrackers. For just an instant I saw fear and bewilderment flicker across his face. No, for this he was not ready. This might well be his day to yield up the ghost. Certainly it would be the longest, most treacherous walk of his career. He was completely surrounded by enemies, the forces of Gog and Magog, people he did not know but who believed they knew him, and what they knew they hated enough to kill. Christ had never encountered rabid crowds like this at Golgotha. Enveloping him on all sides—like devils in a circle of hell created for him alone—twisted white lips spewed obscenities, white fingers clawed through the crowd to tear at his tailored blue suit. Out of nowhere a brick came singing through the air. Dazed, he dropped to his knees. Immediately Jesse Jackson and other Movement lieutenants drawn from the Vice Lords and Saints threw themselves between King and the crowd, forcing his head down until the injured philosopher stopped seeing double, rose again to his feet, rocking a little back and forth on his heels, and whispered more to himself than anyone else, "I'm all right, don't worry about me. I've been hit so many times I'm immune to it. This is what we wanted. Keep moving . . ."

They pushed deeper down streets packed with hysterical white homeowners. Reporters and cameramen from the conservative *Tribune* and *Daily News* darted around them, wearing protective helmets and keeping their heads ducked. King, dwarfed on all sides, blood and sweat spangling his brow, pulled off his tie; he unbuttoned the top of his shirt, and did not so much walk as he was carried forward by the crowd inside a girdle of gang members, all sworn to nonviolence, who hove close to the sidewalks, providing a flesh-

and-blood barrier for the minister's troops to march in rows of eight on pavement hot enough to fry an egg. Then: over the heads of the crowd I saw a knife hurtling toward the minister. The blade, missing King entirely, buried itself in a bystander. The blue-helmeted police saw nothing. They were dodging rocks and debris, hitting the ground en masse, incapable of holding back hecklers whose numbers swelled to five thousand as the marchers stepped over broken glass and at last reached their destination, the Halvorsen agency at 3145 West 63rd Street. There, beneath the company's sign (REAL ESTATE INSURANCE *sales management appraisals*), in front of its long glass window, King, rubbing his forehead, kneeled down to pray.

Amy's voice crackled over my radio. "Matthew, I can't see anything from here! What's going on?"

"They're heading back your way," I said. "Get Chaym into Doc's car—"

"What?"

"Just *do* it!"

Somehow the marchers safely retraced their steps to Marquette Park. In the bedlam of chartered buses and automobiles tearing away, wrecked cars tipped on their sides, their leather interiors blazing, we switched Smith and the minister; Doc rode hunched down in the backseat of the Chevelle to his flat on the West Side, and Smith traveled in the car in which King had come, a gang of whites chasing after him with sticks until the driver put pedal to metal and left them in a cloud of carbon monoxide.

Within minutes of our arrival at South Hamlin Street, no sooner than I had the minister upstairs and Smith back in the Chevelle out of sight with Amy in an alleyway, the apartment and hallway filled with Movement workers, all maneuvering to get the minister's attention. At the kitchen table he sat still shaking from his most recent brush with death, his suitcoat draped over the chair behind him, his shirtcuffs bunched up to his elbows, tie unbraided, and his head canted left as a young woman with skinny legs washed the wound on his forehead, then smoothed a Band-Aid just above and to the right of his eyebrow. While she ministered to him, smacking him lightly on the shoulder when he moved, he smoked cigarettes end-on-end and talked steadily to his captains in the packed room in which two weeks earlier I'd introduced him to Smith.

"I've never seen anything like this." His eyes squeezed shut for a second; the blow to his temple had brought on the worst headache he'd felt in years. "We've been in demonstrations all over the South—Mississippi, Alabama—but I've never seen mobs as full of hate or as hostile as the ones we saw today. Nothing like this!"

One of his staff members, a lean minister standing to his left, agreed. "There is a bright side. The boys you picked from the gangs to be march captains acquitted themselves pretty well."

"Yes . . . yes, you're right. I saw a couple of them with broken noses and bruises"—he rubbed his own nose—"but none of them struck back. Lord, I hope the reporters put that in the newspapers. It proves the opposite of what they've been saying—what Daley and J. H. Jackson said about demonstrations igniting violence on our side."

I interrupted, wanting to tell him about our last two weeks with Smith. But the instant I called his name, he cut me off.

"Matthew, I didn't see you standing there! Do you have a minute? There's something I must speak alone with you about, if you don't mind."

He grabbed his coat and squeezed through a crush of people in the hallway, leading me into the bathroom, then closed the door, which muffled the chattering and constantly ringing phone outside. The minister lowered himself onto the covered toilet seat and, fumbling inside his coat pocket, looked up.

"Sometimes this is the only room where I can go to get a little peace and quiet."

"I understand, sir." (And I did: his namesake, Martin Luther, was reported to have experienced illumination while seated on the throne of Denmark.)

"I'm pleased by how you've handled your project. After the demonstration those hooligans took off after him, not us, and he didn't suffer a scratch. You know, with a little more work this can become a great institution."

King located what he wanted in his coat. An envelope containing five one-hundred-dollar bills for Smith's first month. We'd agreed cash payments would replace checks. There would be no paper trail. No trace of his alter ego's existence.

"He *does* favor me, doesn't he?"

"Yes, sir—even more now than before."

"Do you have other plans for him tonight?"

"Tonight?" I looked at my wrist, realized I didn't have a watch on and was staring at skin, but not knowing what else to do I looked for a full three seconds anyway.

"Around seven, yes," Doc said. "I'd like to send him out to a Negro church in the suburbs—Calvary AME—to pick up an award they're giving me. Do you think he can do that?"

"I'm not . . . sure. This was his first day . . . You can't be there?"

"Oh, maybe, if things settle down here. I'll do my best to get away, but I'd like Chaym there just in case. He won't have to give a speech or anything. Just shake hands and say thank you. Do you think he can handle this? I'd hate to disappoint the parishioners at Reverend Coleman's church who invited me."

"We can try," I said.

Then he wanted to use the bathroom. Stepping back into the hallway, I saw Amy by the front door, not downstairs at the car where I'd left her and asked specifically that she take care of Chaym. I could tell she'd been crying. I led her outside to the stairs, away from the others, and asked, "What's wrong?"

"Chaym kicked me out of the car. Matthew, he can be *terrible* sometimes!" Amy leaned into my shoulder and cried a little more. I closed my eyes, inhaling her perfume, feeling her fingers on my chest, her belly against mine. Instinctively, as I held my breath, both my hands lifted to pull her closer, but I resisted that impulse, and simply stood motionless until she was cried out and moved away, wiping her eyes. "Sometimes I'd like to *hit* him, except it'd feel like hitting Dr. King."

"Okay," I said, "what's bothering him? Everything went perfectly."

"Yes, but it's not what he wants now. He says we're treating him like a clay pigeon. A decoy. Chaym says he's better than that, as good as King any day, and he wants a chance to prove it."

"Maybe he's got it."

"Huh?"

"I'll explain later. You said he's still in the car?"

"Last time I looked, but—"

I was halfway down the stairs before she finished, pushing through a crowd at the door and SCLC workers holding them back. I circled round the block to where we'd left the Chevelle, but I was thinking of Amy, how warm and soft she'd felt in the crook of my arm. I'd wanted badly to hold her. Problem was, the fool I'd made of myself in the farmhouse was green in my memory, and I decided I could be satisfied with just being there, asking for nothing, if she needed my shoulder, or a hand to hold, or someone to listen. Out-casts, I'd learned from Chaym (though perhaps he failed at this himself), learned not to ask for much, yet were there if the Abelites were in need.

I walked up behind the Chevelle and saw Smith so absorbed in what he was doing he failed to hear my footsteps approaching. He was rummaging, I realized, through his suitcoat. Then he found what he was looking for. A small case containing a hypodermic needle wrapped in cotton. Smith tore off his coat, unbuttoned the left cuff of his shirt, and rolled back the sleeve. He jabbed his fingers along the length of his forearm, found a likely spot, and held the nee-dle up, pushing out its air bubble. I watched him lick a spot on his forearm wet and shiny with spittle; then he broke skin with the needle and, his eyes heavily lidded, he watched thin fluid vanish from the needle into his vein.

He replaced the needle in its case, put that in the jacket pocket, dropped his head back on the car's vinyl seat, and let his tortured mind dream. For a long time I did not move; I did not wish to interrupt him, for without dreams, even drug-induced ones, all a black man has left are nightmares. After I got hold of myself, I walked to his window and knocked with my knuckles on the glass.

"Doc says he needs us tonight. You up for that, Chaym?"

He sniffed and nodded. "I'm good."

"I'll bet. Can you accept an award for him?"

"Hell yeah, I'm ready to do *any*thing."

"You want to talk?"

"What the fuck about? You wanna talk to somebody, Bishop, go to confession."

I let that ride, easing onto the front seat beside him, resolving to say nothing of what I'd seen to either Doc or Amy. As long as he could do the job, and cover the minister's back if a gig went sour, who was I, after all, to cast the first stone?

7

Calvary AME Church, a pitched-roof, redbrick building with
two lancet-arched doorways and a blue and white sign swinging from its southwest edge on the corners of Emerson and
Darrow streets in the quiet, progressive suburb of Evanston,
was plain and inconspicuous enough for travelers to completely miss—like so much in the black world—if they
weren't looking for it. Its rich, never recorded history was
hidden inside, stored within every parishioner, or so Amy said
that evening after the Marquette march as we sped down the
Outer Drive, crossing bustling Howard Street into a sleepy
suburb quite different from south or west Chicago. The riots
and agony of marching in the city had largely bypassed the
cultural island of Evanston. Most black residents were too
busy making a living and caring for their children to take a
day off for civil disobedience, though they cared deeply

about the Movement's northern campaign and cheered King, the rebel messiah, the almost paradoxical fusion of Cain and Abel, when the Chicago campaign put into practice his ingenious method of "creative tension" aimed at disrupting the status quo by forcing long-buried hatreds to surface, where they were exposed for the world to see. King's philosophy notwithstanding, "creative tension" was an act of violence, the murder of a repressive past so that a new order—God's order—could be born. Yet Evanston, while not the fabled Promised Land, was a curious pocket of tranquillity compared to the Black Belt. There, residents could walk safely at night from one end of town to the other. Liquor was not sold—for that you had to drive to Skokie. There were white millionaires, blue-collar black homeowners bonded by church affiliations, an integrated school system, stores and movie theaters (three), and some years the best public high school in the nation. (However, the school superintendent did demand parental permission on both sides before he would condone interracial dating.)

Because Mama Pearl, once an employee of Fanny's Restaurant in Evanston, occasionally attended services with friends at Calvary AME, Amy knew something of the town's older black residents, mostly craftsmen—plumbers and electricians—transplanted from the South during World War II, whole families that migrated up the Illinois Central Railroad from the Mississippi Delta, from Tennessee and Arkansas and western Kentucky in the greatest mass movement of humanity in American history. They were, in their own way, initially outcasts. Their church, started in Philadelphia in 1787 after the Great Awakening by Richard Allen, was equidistant from the ivied halls and manicured lawns of Northwestern University and the all-black Center Hospital, situated on the canal dividing Evanston from lily-white Skokie. According to Amy's mother, nearly half the church's teenagers came into the world at Center Hospital, and each could claim a single, courageous black woman, Dr. Jennifer Hale, as the person who saw them before their own mothers and spanked wind into their lungs. Amy said that decades earlier when Hale, a beautiful, buff-colored young doctor with the gentility one associates with Creoles, arrived in Evanston, she discovered that black patients were turned away from the doors of Evanston's white hospital farther north near Wilmette, regardless of how sick they might be. Segregation forced Hale to ferry her patients to hospitals on Chicago's South Side, and too many died on the way for her to rest with this disastrous arrangement. She was outraged. Her patients, while pariahs to the white population, worked in white homes and saved to send their children to college— that, after forming their own neighborhood YMCA and colored Boy and Girl Scout chapters; some held down three jobs a week, always struggling and sacrificing to free their sons and daughters from the curse of color that hung over their own lives. The idea of public assistance was anathema to many of them, such a blow to their southern pride that they never considered for a moment turning outside their own families—or extended families—for help. They treated all the black children at Calvary AME as their own, scolding them and telling their parents if in public they behaved in ways that reflected badly on the struggling community as a whole.

By mobilizing blacks and whites of conscience, Hale became one of the principal players in first envisioning, then coaxing into being, Center Hospital; and by doing this, Amy said, she saved countless black lives as well as created jobs for other doctors, nurses, and dentists of color. The hospital, though never as large or as well-funded as its white counterpart, was nevertheless something of a beacon of pride for local blacks in the 1950s, and Dr. Hale justly held a place of high esteem in Evanston. Her life was her work. She never married, but she delivered countless baby boomers after the war—her "children," she called them—and many were pleasantly shocked to realize that Hale recognized them by name twenty years later as she traveled from one Evanston home to another, making house calls.

Among her elderly patients, those belonging to the first black wave that migrated to Evanston, was a congenial black contractor named Robert Jackson whose company won the contract for building Calvary AME, and who, even after the white hospital began accepting Negro patients, remained loyal to Center and allowed his relations to take him nowhere else. They belonged to the same era, Dr. Hale and contractor Jackson—a breed of black men and women, like King's parents and Amy's great-grandfather, so toughened by prejudice, by the rule of having to do twice as much as whites to get half as far, that they regarded no problem as insurmountable. With little formal education, he'd come north from a farm near Abbeville in South Carolina during the 1920s, bringing nothing more with him than a strong back, a quick wit, and a burning need to succeed against staggering odds; he checked out Chicago, then moved to Evanston, where Negroes found leftovers from the tables of well-to-do whites somewhat larger than the scraps tossed to blacks in the city. No question, there was a residue of apartheid here. Black women, when cleaning some white homes, were likely to find literature from the John Birch Society on the living room coffee tables. But where others saw only racial restrictions and what they couldn't do, Jackson, a tall, dark-fired man who was most certainly a follower of Booker T. Washington, believed in his bones that opportunities had to be made by Negroes if they were to happen at all. Was the hospital segregated? Did Northwestern's sororities exclude blacks in their charters? Were white milk companies denying service to colored folks who settled in Evanston after their long sojourn from Georgia, Louisiana, and Alabama? Always a man who preferred work and getting his hands dirty to complaining, building to bellyaching, Bob Jackson responded to racism by founding the Jackson Dairy Company. Every morning before daybreak he delivered on black doorsteps milk in pint bottles of thick, sturdy glass that bore his name on the front and on the back the reminder *This bottle not sold . . . Wash and Return.* He labored to put his business in the black (no pun intended, Amy said), came up with a catchy jingle for it, and did well enough, thank you, until the Depression brought it abruptly to an end, but not by any means his restlessness, ambition, and sense of industry.

Construction work came next, mainly as a way to make ends meet, though Bob Jackson was never satisfied, according to what Amy'd learned from her grandmother, working for other people. He stayed on the crew long enough to learn the ropes, then ventured out on his own again, this time unveiling yet another dream that had him up pacing the floor at night and pulling his hair, the little he had in his late fifties. By name, the dream was the Jackson Construction Company. And his first act as an entrepreneur was to offer jobs to the sons of his brothers down South. The elder Jackson's new business thrived for decades, drawing on a pool of black subcontractors who helped him raise churches, apartment complexes, and residences—places for his people to live and worship their god—all over the North Shore, including the two-story, many-roomed building he built for himself in the heart of the black community on Simpson Street, with rental spaces on the first floor for a beauty parlor and a barbershop.

The product of his labor made Bob Jackson a proud man well enough off to buy a bench for his family at Calvary

AME, where his nieces sang in the choir; for despite obstacles and a hundred white men who'd stood in his way (and were now deservedly long forgotten, with no monuments on the landscape to mark *their* existence), he could boast that his blood *built* this town. With many black Evanstonians he shared the belief that life was getting better, that their offerings to the Lord had been blessed a hundredfold since they left the South, and with legal segregation struck down he counseled his platoon of grand-nephews and -nieces (spared the devastating discrimination he'd known) that if they were genuinely concerned about the economic inequities they saw in the world, "The best thing you children can do for the poor is not be one of them." On the surface it sounded harsh, but his relations knew their great-uncle meant something else, that by fulfilling his duties as a householder, by creating wealth, he always had deep pockets into which their fathers and mothers could reach for funds when they needed the down payment on a home, or extra cash to cover their bills when they were between jobs. Bob Jackson paid his grand-nieces and -nephews four dollars for every A they received at Noyes Elementary School and Skiles Junior High, three dollars for every B (nothing for a C), and established a trust fund they could draw upon for college tuition because more than anything else he wanted them to have the one thing he lacked in 1966 that kept him from becoming a millionaire. "Get an education," he told them. "Don't you put anything ahead of that."

Smith was scrunched down in the backseat of the Chevelle, allowing Amy to apply a Band-Aid to exactly the spot on his forehead where the minister was struck by a brick. "That's who's coming to this church tonight?" He was still high, sailing on heroin. His voice trembled. "People like them?"

"Probably," Amy said. "People like Mr. Jackson's kin, Dr. Hale, and Leroy Young. He rewired the bookstore, Great

Expectations, over near the university. They don't make headlines. They're just proud, quietly pious, good people. Like the folks in Doc's community in Atlanta." She gazed out the window at palatial homes perched far back from the road on Ridge Avenue. "They're the ones who want to honor Doc. I'm pretty sure Elijah Muhammad would bomb here."

"You didn't tell me any of this before I said I'd do it."

"Why?" she asked. "Does it matter?"

"Yeah, it matters. Everything here seems so . . . *finished*. God loves these Negroes. What do I *say* to them?"

"Nothing!" I whirled round in my seat, grabbed his tie, and pulled his head toward me. "You don't say a blessed thing, Chaym, you hear me? That's not what we're here for." I almost lost control of the steering wheel, so I let his tie go, and took a deep breath to steady myself. "Besides, I don't think you're ready. Just accept the goddamn prize for Doc and get down off the pulpit as soon as you can. Tell the pastor you're tired. Tell him you've got laryngitis. Tell him *any-thing*, but wrap this up as fast as you can. If you don't, you'll ruin everything. Got that?"

"You don't think I'm good enough to give a speech here?"

"I didn't say that."

"But it's what you *meant*," he grumbled. "Shit, as long as *he's* alive, I guess I'll always be nothing."

Amy cleared her throat to end the conversation. "Matthew, look in the rearview mirror."

"Why?"

"Just *look*, will you?"

I cranked down my window and in the mirror affixed to the door saw a plain green Plymouth about five car-lengths behind us.

"Those Wise Guys," said Smith, "have been baby-sittin' us since we left Doc's apartment. I recognize the plates. That's a government car . . ."

Amy pressed her nose against the back window. "Why're they following us?"

"I'll give you three guesses," said Smith, "and the first two don't count. You gonna call this off?"

"No." I slowed the car to a crawl. "I think I can circle around the block and lose them."

Amy shook my shoulder. "Are you kiddin'? The church is straight ahead and—oh no, will you—will you *look* at that?"

The entire block from Dodge Avenue to Darrow was cordoned off. Vans from local radio and television stations were parked alongside the church, closed in by a crowd I estimated to be at five or six hundred. A traffic cop, young, still wearing his sunglasses though it was twilight, waved vehicles west up Emerson Street toward Skokie. I slowed the Chevelle even more, rolled down my window, told the cop I was bringing the minister for tonight's service, then turned right toward the church when he let me through. The green Plymouth eased toward the curb at the end of the block. Sunlight was fading fast. I couldn't clearly see the faces of the men following us, and then there was no time to think about them because Calvary AME's pastor, Rev. Jacob Coleman, a tidy-looking, tea-colored man with a chrysanthemum in his buttonhole who'd been waiting inside the door, rushed outside. He took Smith by the arm, explaining that his ushers would provide security, and led us through people trying to touch or detain the man they thought was King to the rear of the church.

Inside a tiny kitchen behind the main room, Smith began to unravel. I should have seen it coming. I should have known. When the magnitude of what the minister asked us to do finally dawned on him, when he was at last standing at the door of his first real performance as a double, Smith collapsed heavily onto a wooden folding chair and began mopping his forehead with a handkerchief. His breathing was ragged, asthmatic. Suddenly he began hiccuping uncontrollably, almost strangling, and looked helplessly toward Amy. I knew she was thinking the same as me. It was over. He was ready for riding in decoy cars, for drawing fire away from King, but not for standing before an audience of over five hundred of the genuinely faithful . . . He was going to crash and burn, as he'd always done in the Citivas Dei. Blow this operation wide open. Fall on his face and embarrass us all. Or worse, pass out right there in the kitchen in front of Calvary AME's ushers and clergy.

"Is something wrong?" Rev. Coleman asked.

Amy eased herself between the pastor and Smith. "Give us a few minutes alone, okay? He just needs to compose himself before he gets his cue."

Reluctantly Rev. Coleman cleared the kitchen, leaving Amy and Smith to themselves.

I left through a side door and joined the congregation, taking a spot to the right of the pulpit. I scanned the crowd, my eyes tracking packed wooden pews in the northeast corner to the laity filling the seats and aisles in front of me, men in their best (and only) dark suits brought out from the back of their closets every Sunday or for occasions such as this, their brogans shined and buffed the night before, cooling themselves with fans provided on the back of each bench, their wives, bearing names such as Adella, Inell, and Luberta, sitting quietly beside them in light cotton dresses, some wearing gloves despite the heat of bodies packed so close together on the benches, perspiration just beginning to bead on their foreheads, dampening at the root oil-heavy hairdos subjected earlier in the day to the straightening comb; I picked out Robert Jackson, a dignified, immaculately dressed, balding Negro sitting on the bench he bought at Calvary, then to his right another old man in a rimpled K-Mart suit, holding a wide-brimmed hat on his lap. My eyes moved up, up above them, to a triptych of stained-glass windows on the western wall, one depicting an alb-clad Jesus standing before Herod's jeering soldiers in the praetorium, another showing Jesus during his lonely vigil of fasting in the desert, the large middle painting portraying a mob hanging him from the cross, and though I knew I was supposed to be watching the crowd, scanning the room every few seconds, my eyes never resting anywhere for long because who knew where an assassin might appear, the feeling that always flooded through me when I entered Negro churches came over me again—the sense, right or wrong, that for the briefest of moments I was safe from the ravages, the irreality, the racial stupidities of the world outside Calvary's doors, that no harm could befall anyone here where so much of value was preserved, meaning made manifest in the minutest details by black people who came to this place, sacred and set off from the chaos of the streets outside, to find husbands and wives, to baptize their children, and to bury their dead before gathering at the home of the deceased, sharing memories of her with the survivors, and being fed by her friends and neighbors who filled the kitchen table with food as a reminder that the bereaved must take nourishment, no matter if they were hungry or not, and walk on, and know that death was not final, because Jesus conquered that once and for all, so yes, eat and be joyful even in mourning because no Christian should forget the good news of the gospel, and no believer in Him ever feel alone or have cause for despair. From my childhood came a verse, *Nevermore thou needest seek Me / I am with thee everywhere: / Raise the stone and thou shalt find Me / Cleave the wood and I am there.* This was what Calvary's congregation believed. What I had been taught from the time I could walk. Religion (Latin *religare,* "to bind," or bring together those things broken, torn asunder). But was all this, I wondered, an illusion?

Badly I wanted to believe, as they did. Behind me I heard twenty teenage girls in white blouses and black skirts blending their voices in the opening hymn, "Amazing Grace," wringing that song out so thoroughly it outstripped anything on WVON's "Top Forty." An old woman who favored Helen Martin about the face stroked the keys of an ancient piano, and while I did not know if her faith was ill-founded, I did know it was here—and only here, in the Negro church, for the last hundred years—that black people pooled their money in order to send the congregation's best students on to train at schools like Morehouse and Fisk; here that teachers selflessly used their weekends and nights to tutor children and conduct Sunday-school classes that, beginning with the Bible, branched out forward and back in the better seminars to examine the preconditions for Christianity and all the intellectual and scientific traditions it had influenced from Tertullian to quantum physics; here that a young Romare Bearden encountered the cornucopia of styles and forms—in spirituals, hymns, prayers, and sermons—that opened him to the epic dialogue that was art; and here, finally, that the civil rights movement was nurtured and sustained, prayer and racial politics inseparably melded by clergy, stewards, and trustees who, if they knew nothing else, understood that they served their people best by reminding them again and again that their political and racial struggles were but the backdrop against which a far greater spiritual odyssey was unfolding, and that no worldly triumph deserved hallelujahs if in their secular victories they somehow lost their souls.

At Calvary's crowded entrance I saw the Wise Guys.

There were two of them, one a hairless, pursy, middle-aged little man in horn-rimmed glasses, slow-moving as a turtle, his belly bubbling over his belt. The other was Titian-haired, thin, in his twenties, his profile made birdlike by a hawkbill nose, carrying a notepad he scribbled on in short-hand, never looking down at the page. They looked tired; they kept shifting their weight from one leg to the other, as if maybe their feet hurt. In another context they might have been Mormons working a neighborhood, tramping from door to door. These were the ones who followed us from the West Side, whom I'd seen on the road in rural Illinois, and who now no doubt were taking down names. They looked intensely interested when the audience rose to its feet and erupted into clapping and cheers.

Amy walked in behind King—it most certainly was King, not Chaym Smith—from the kitchen to a row of seats on the stage. I had no idea how the minister had gotten here at the last minute, but I muttered thanks to the Almighty, for the prayer I'd made had come to pass, and I released my breath, which I felt I'd been holding for hours.

And then the audience settled down. Whether the minister knew it or not, his physical presence, while not imposing, brought a hush like soft background music, or as if someone cracked a window in a crowded, smoke-filled room. I felt something in him sorely lacking in myself—grace or a spiritual wealth so great he could give of himself endlessly, and always there was twelve basketfuls left over, as one might dip a cup into the sea and never see it emptied. He was an old soul. Centuries old. Not putting on a show, he stopped all conversation and commanded respect; not justifying himself, he was distinguished; not boasting, he was instantly acknowledged. Standing beside Rev. Coleman at the forest of black microphones on the pulpit, with flashbulbs explod-ing like fireworks in the hands of the Associated Press and British newsmen who rushed to the front of the church, he was august, hugely present, relaxed, munificent, established in mercy, but at his center I felt a cemetery—a coolness and crypt—in which all regard for himself and his safety lay buried. Something in him was dead, extinguished so long ago during the Montgomery boycott when he was hardly more than a boy that it no longer even existed in memory. In some way that I could not coax into clarity, his very presence challenged me and commented, without his having yet said a word, on my own staggering shortcomings as a man, a Negro, a Christian. The level he was living on did that. No newspaper article or television interview touched what I felt that evening. To engage him at all, this preacher who dared to say, "There will be no permanent end to the race problem until oppressed men develop the capacity to love their enemies," who quoted Epictetus, Keats, Emerson, and Dunbar as if they were his first cousins—to meet him face-to-face, I realized, forced a man to kick up his own thoughts and feelings a notch or two, as you might when going one-on-one with the finest athletes on a playing field, so that even mediocre men like me rose momentarily to finer planes of performance.

"It is with great pleasure," said Rev. Coleman, "that I present this Achievement Award to you from the grateful membership of Calvary AME Church." He handed a heavy plaque, gold lettering engraved on black, to the minister and shook his hand vigorously; then, smiling, Coleman turned the ceremony over to King.

I should have been watching the crowd, but I could not wrench my eyes away as King, the portrait of composure that evening, despite all he'd endured only hours earlier, placed the plaque to one side on a small table of flowers, his movements as flawless as those of a fish, his fingers seeming to merge with the surface of the pulpit. More than any place else, he was at home there, in the pulpit, leaning into the microphones, having preached since his teens beside his father, and then during his college years in the Baptist churches of King Senior's friends in Boston and throughout the South, incorporating the best of what he learned from Mays and Brightman in their classrooms into sermons he thrilled audiences with—in his early twenties—the very next Sunday. How had he put it in one sermon? "As a young man with most of my life ahead of me, I decided to give my life to something eternal and absolute. Not to these little gods that are here today and gone tomorrow. But to God who is the same yesterday, today, and forever." He never knew—could never know—exactly what the room he was to speak in would look like. For the briefest of instants, the length of an Amen, he adjusted his voice to the room's unique acoustics and the placement of the stage. He got through these engagements, for which he was paid between $500 and $1,000, by focusing exclusively on the present moment, living completely in the here, the now, oblivious to whatever programs he had scheduled for the next day, willfully forgetful of how well or poorly he'd done before. His experience of time was reduced, on the road, to seriality, fully lived moments—like islands—separate from one another: he was *here* (Chicago) and *here* (Jamaica) and *here* (Paris) with little bridge between locations. Some days it felt as if his life dissolved or abruptly cut from place to place, as in a film.

Fortunately, he didn't truly need notes anymore. He'd done this so often before that he could speak for two hours or three without once looking down. The quotations he needed were permanently imprinted in his memory. All he need do was "switch," as he put it to himself, into a public mode, and the words, one whole structured paragraph after another, came pouring out of him. In his teens, when speaking became effortless this way, he'd wonder after an event, "Did I really do that?" because his public self had seemed so different to him, like a mask; but then he realized some few years later that man and mask were fused. His private self *was* the mask. The Movement left no room for subjectivity; inner and outer were the same.

"Thank you . . . thank you very much," he said as he glanced around the church, making visual contact with everyone, including those crammed into the balconies. "A moment ago, Reverend Coleman asked me if I was disillusioned after today's march. He asked me if I felt we were wrong to come to Chicago, and what did I make of the hatred we saw in Marquette Park. Now, I can't lie to you. I was stunned. In every one of those screaming white faces I saw hatred that obliterated the last vestiges of humanity. I saw sickness and evil brought on by segregation and sin-ruined lives. Because, you see, those people were living in fear. They were afraid that accepting Negroes as their neighbors—or anybody different—meant they'd lose their homes, their jobs, their place in society, possibly even their sons and daughters in marriage to people who don't look the way they do. They feared losing their sense of self, and we all know that's the most powerful fear on earth, the one that fuels all the others. Fear, I've been told, is a drug—it releases peptide hormones that have the same pharmacologic characteristics as opium. You could say that anyone experiencing fear is narcoticized, not in his right mind, mesmerized, in the constant state of hypnosis so many metaphysicians tell us is the human condition. That's what I saw today. People throwing bricks at phantoms. Shouting at shadows, since there are *no* Negroes, and whites either, except of course in their own deluded minds . . .

"After liberating lunch counters, winning court battles and homes in nice neighborhoods, we must in our next campaign free consciousness itself from fear, from what William Blake called 'mind-forg'd manacles.' But to do this we must unlearn many things. We must be quiet and not deluded or deceived by the creations of our own minds. The soil of the soul must be plowed. Reverend Coleman"—he squinted behind him at the pastor sitting rapt beside Amy—"the answer to your question is that no man can bring me so low as to make me hate him, no matter what we ran up against today in Chicago, because hate is based on fear, and I don't fear losing anything since I willingly gave up everything to the one I love."

The audience sang back, "Preach!"

"That's right," he went on, raising his right hand to tug at his earlobe, light spinning off his simple wedding band, "I've got nothing to lose. Nothing to fear because after being in the storm so long I've learned to accept only one problem: What is God? Every night when I get down on my knees to pray or close my eyes in quiet meditation I'm holding a funeral for the self. I'm digging a little grave for the ego. I'm saying, like the lovely Catholic nun I read about who works with the poor in Calcutta, that I will despoil myself of all that is not God; I will strip my heart of every created thing; I will live in poverty and detachment; I will renounce my will, my inclinations, my whims and fancies, and make myself a willing servant of the will of God. As Whitehead might put it, 'I am' is an example of Misplaced Concreteness. And what's left when you get the I out of the way? Only the others, living and dead, who are *already* so thoroughly integrated into our lives you can never get rid of them. No, the segregationists lost before they even began. Nothing stands alone. You know, not one member of the White Citizens' Council can finish breakfast in the morning without relying on the rest of the world. That sponge 'Bull' Connor bathes with came from the Pacific Islands. His towel was spun in Turkey. The coffee Orval Faubus drinks traveled all the way from South America, the tea from China, the cocoa from West Africa. And every time George Wallace or Malcolm X writes his name he's using ink evolved from India and an alphabet inherited from the Romans, who derived it from the Greeks after they'd borrowed it from Phoenicians, who received their symbols from Seirites living on the Sinai peninsula between Egypt and Palestine . . . After a time, I tell you, a man comes to see only a We, this precious moment as a tissue in time holding past, future, and present, with all of us in the red, everlasting debtors—ontological thieves—in a universe of interrelatedness . . . Every man and woman is a speculum, our mirror. Our twin."

Shivers played across my shoulders. The more I listened and looked, the more I suspected that it was Smith, not King, at the microphone, speaking to all gathered, yes, but in a way not to us at all—or, more exactly, to the spirit immanent in each parishioner, offering his speech as a form of sacrifice, holding nothing back, forgetting himself utterly in the demands of the moment and allowing the Father within him to doeth the work and the Father within us to receive it.

"Think about it." He stroked his chin now, continuing without notecards or a single piece of paper in front of him. "We do everything we can to avoid facing ourselves and, by virtue of that, the real structure of reality, which Sir James Jeans, the physicist, tells us is more like a great thought than a machine driven by matter. Sir Arthur Eddington put it just as succinctly, saying—if I remember this right—'The external world of physics has become a world of shadows. In removing our illusions we remove substance, for indeed we have seen that substance is one of the greatest of our illusions.' Yet and still, most of us have carnal minds. Crude minds. We forget that nothing burns in hell except self-will. We seldom, if ever, think four-dimensionally. Lord, we hate to think at all, judging by how we spend our time. By the time most of you are sixty-five years old, you will have looked at 102,000 hours of television, heard 25,000 hours of radio, seen 300,000 comic pages and 3,599 movies, drunk 18,000 bottles of beer and 3,000 fifths of whiskey . . . and never devoted one hour to meditating on the truth that whatever is done to the least of us is done to all, and to the Lord we say we love. If you believe in Jesus, then you believe in the man who sleeps outside your door on the street. The single woman struggling to feed her children. The worker deprived of his job. You believe in the brokenhearted, the poor, the unemployed, the captive, the blind, the bruised. And all the countless outcasts tossed to one side by a society that values profits more than it does people. But I know that at the numinous heart of being, there is a Heart, a Father who, if we approach the poor by one span, will come to us by one cubit; if we move toward the needy one cubit, He draws nearer by a fathom; if we love all men as our brothers, He embraces us with a redemption greater than any fortune in the world. Brothers and sisters, Reverend Coleman, no man can make me hate. I have no choice but to love others because I *am* the others. Reason (to say nothing of self-interest) demands that I care for them as much as I do for myself.

"I should stop now, I suppose. A wise man once said, 'Speech is always the great-grandson of truth' . . . Thank you, and God bless you for your kindness."

He back pedaled from the pulpit and bowed. Throughout the church there was silence. Moments later, thunderous applause. Parishioners sprang to their feet, throwing paper fans and programs into the air, shouting, pressing toward the stage. The older of the Wise Guys was talking to someone on his two-way radio, plugging his ear with one finger to muffle the calls for the speaker to give them more. I broke free from the spell his words had woven and scrambled from my position, heading back to the kitchen to congratulate Smith— once he pulled away from his admirers—on a stunning sermon that would have made King proud. But as I pushed open the side door, I saw our charge standing off to one side in the shadows—like a shadow himself, staring up at the stage where the parishioners hugged King (it had been him after all), shook his hand, posed to be in photos beside him, and clamored for his autograph. Who could doubt that this man had won his wings, his seat in Glory? Smith watched with perfect, everyman impotence and awe the love and admiration showered on his famous twin, seeing the Good but powerless to be it, lost in his littleness, and to me it seemed King's double was undergoing a kind of living death in the great man's presence, despite his intense training and desire to be remembered by God. Obviously, His children did not see Chaym in the shadows. Nor, I thought, would they ever.

I went to his side, placing my hand on his shoulder. Smith dropped his eyes, staring at his feet, almost as if he was ashamed of—and despised—his own being. "How does he *do* that?" He was not, I saw, talking to me. "Some of the things he said . . . That was *my* stuff. Not things I've ever said, but stuff I've felt. Like my spirit is trapped in his, which is so much clearer and bigger and cleaner. His voice . . . It feels when he's preaching like his words come from inside *me*, not outside—like he gives my soul a voice. It doesn't make sense . . ."

"C'mon," I said. "I think we better go. It's been a long day. We can stay at my apartment in the city tonight." I asked Amy to bring the Chevelle around back, then nudged Smith toward the rear of the church so we could exit unseen, and I was so exhausted from the day's events that I failed to notice the old man in the wrinkled K-Mart suit until he was upon us, and I was staring at a clump of brown clay with two chips of glass stuck in the center: his eyes. His cheap suit fit him miserably. His trousers dropped like drapery, not touching his wing tips but riding above his ankles and black socks so old the elastic was gone, leaving one, his left, bunched around his shoelaces. And he looked worse than his suit, sick and senile. I placed his age at seventy. Seventy-five.

"Reverend," he said, extending a dithering, arthritic hand toward Smith, "I took the El all the way from the West Side to hear your speech 'cause I need to tell you somethin', sir—"

"Not now," I said. "I'm sorry, old-timer, but we're a little tired this evening."

"It's all right, Bishop." Smith took the old man's palsied hand, like the tongue of a worn shoe to the touch, and shook it. "Maybe I can help this gentleman. Your place is on the West Side, right? He can ride in back with me, then you can drop him off. That way he can tell us what's on his mind . . ." He winked at me. "It's what *he'd* do, right? You can't turn anybody away."

When Amy pulled up in the car, the old man bent over and climbed onto the backseat, sandwiching himself between Smith and me, his knees nearly touching his chin as he prepared to state his business and, unbeknownst to us, propel Chaym Smith toward the last stage of his evolution.

8

"Luther King, I've been tryin' to get to you for twelve years."
From Dodge Avenue to Howard Street, the old man sat
hunched between us, the corners of his mouth tucked in, his
fists closed tight on his knees. His stomach rumbled now
and then, like thunder. You'd have thought he'd forgotten we
were in the car. Every so often he coughed with a deep, rattling sound and held his chest. Neither Amy nor I could
prompt him to say what was wrong, and to be perfectly honest I was afraid he might have heart failure right there in the
backseat of the car. Smith pressed his fingers to his lips, sig-
naling us not to rush him, to let the old man take as much
time as he needed. There were burn scars on his wrists and
the back of his hands; part of his right thumb was missing,
stumped off by, I supposed, an industrial or down-home
farming accident.

At last, after blowing his nose again—two ringing toots and a rest—and sticking his thumb in his mouth to line up his teeth, the old man said, "You don't know me, but I know who *you* are." He reached into his suitcoat and removed a black leather wallet. Out of that he pulled two dog-eared black-and-white photographs and passed them to Smith. In one snapshot, he, as a younger man, posed against the Ferris wheel and booths of the St. Louis World's Fair, his arm encircling a black woman of catastrophic beauty: sloe-black eyes, high cheekbones, hair falling on her shoulders and along the tight lace collar of her dress. A second photo presented the same woman in a wedding dress, her waist so small a man could make a circle with his hands around it. She was smiling shyly at the camera, caught by surprise, cutting a three-tiered cake with two colored figurines on the top layer, and for a moment I was startled by how she favored Smith. Looking at our passenger again, comparing his features to Chaym's when we passed streetlights that briefly lit the car's interior, I was all but certain he was Smith's father.

"That's my Ida," said the old man. "We got married in nineteen twenty-three. Let me tell you, this city was the place to be in the twenties. Ida loved dancin' in them clubs on Saturday night. And the music? It's like they say, Reverend. Back then a peckerwood woulda give anythin' to be a colored man on the weekends. But that was 'fore the war come along and times got tighter'n Dick's hatband . . . We joint the Moorish Zionist Temple along about then. The first year we was there the leader of that temple run off with my wife."

"I'm sorry." Smith handed back his photos just as we reached the address he'd given as his home, the Hotel Sutherland on lower Wabash, a flophouse where beds rented for a dollar a night, in a neighborhood of abandoned cars stripped of their antennas and tires, where steam issued from open sewers, sidewalks were shattered into mosaics of white cement, bow-tied Muslims waved *Muhammad Speaks,* panhandlers wearing do-rags under porkpie hats hawked cheap watches banded from their bony wrists to their fore-arms, and the stain of industrial smoke and soot spread across broken windows, broken doors, and broken walls scrawled with the graffiti of street gangs. "I can see that hurt you a great deal. I could say a prayer for you—"

"Don't bother." The old man stepped out onto the curb when I opened the rear door and held it for him. "I don't want nothin' anymore. Y'all took it all. Ministers like you are responsible for all my troubles."

My scalp trembled when he said that. Where, I won-dered, had I heard those words before. And then—too late!—I knew: Izola Curry had said just that before stabbing King.

From inside his coat the old man withdrew a nickel-plated, Colt semiautomatic, pointing the ancient pistol straight-armed at Smith, who instinctively threw up his left hand and tried to turn away. The old man pulled the trigger over and over, pumping five rounds into the backseat. The muzzle flash blinded me; then I saw Smith dancing like a marionette on the cushion as the old man emptied his gun, firing, spiderwebbing the windows, frosting them with bul-lets that ricocheted crazily around the car like bees. Amy dived under the dashboard. Brass casings rained on the roof of the Chevelle, the curb, and one, burning hot, seared my forehead. Pedestrians were ducking into doorways. After the first shot, my ears were cottoned. Deaf. Sounds were muted like voices submerged in the sea, and all I remember after I froze was the old man bolting into the hotel, leaping over a derelict sprawled dead drunk in the lobby, and Amy, her hair sopping with blood, cranking the starter and Smith yelling at me to get the hell into the car and at her to drive to the Nest.

"No!" I was leaning over him, unclear how I'd climbed back into the moving car. "You need a doctor." Blood spread on his white dress shirt. The seat cushions. On me. The back of the car was peppered with bullet holes. The floor littered with hot casings. The air thick with the sweet, pungent odor of gunpowder. The blood in back was enough for a butchering.

Smith, holding his side, tried to sit up, then stopped. "Ho, Lawd! That *hurts*!"

"We have to find a hospital—"

"Been in too many hospitals. I don't wanna see no more hospitals long as I live."

"How about a mortician? That's what you'll need if we don't get you to Cook County."

"Fine, but *no* hospitals."

Already his eyes were starting to slick over, to blur. He was slipping into shock. "Do like I said. I been shot at before. That jacket'll stop the bleeding."

"Matthew!" Though she was yelling, I could barely hear her. "We *have* to get him to a doctor."

"Do what he wants. It's his life."

She made a sound not to be deciphered.

I tore off my jacket, tied it around the entrance and exit wounds. With my palms I kept applying pressure until the bleeding subsided. By then, Smith had passed out. But before he lost consciousness, he'd been thinking more clearly than Amy or I. Hospitals were risky. There would be too many questions. Too many police. Too many reporters saying the minister had been shot by . . . another black man. How the Chicago campaign's opponents would love *that*. We needed time to regroup. Amy headed for the freeway. I thought *she* was about to go into shock, barreling down Route 51, driving on adrenaline. She squeezed one fist into her mouth to keep from crying. Outside Champaign, she stopped to give me the wheel when the image of the pistol firing repeatedly rose up unbidden in her mind, forcing her to the side of the road. She cut off the engine and sobbed. "I *never* thought this would happen. I can't *do* this. I can't."

I climbed into the driver's seat, though I was hardly in better shape than she (sounds still came to me flattened, as if from far away). In Pinckneyville we stopped for bandage compresses, gauze, items to fight off infection. "Listen," I said, "if not for Chaym, that could have been Doc tonight."

Shortly after daybreak I pulled up in front of the farmhouse. We were tired. Wired. Yet even before we reached the porch, shouldering Smith on both sides, I sensed that something at the Nest was wrong. Footprints not our own led up the front stairs. The door, which I'd locked, was cracked open. Cautiously I kicked it with my heel, and we entered disheveled rooms that looked as if they'd been visited by the Israeli Mossad, followed by the Tontons Macoutes. I thought something in the house had exploded. Clothing was tossed everywhere. Files confettied the floor. Bookshelves were overturned. Cabinets and Mama Pearl's tables were broken. Amidst this wreckage of her grandmother's belongings, Amy was silent. And not to be consoled. She looked round the room with something like resignation, slowly and quietly uprighting a steeple-backed chair topped with a wooden fleur-de-lis, and I knew at that moment we had lost her. I got Smith into bed. After washing his wound, I took the first watch, standing vigil over him all that day as he slept.

Quite possibly, that was the longest day of my life. The old man was a bad shot. Only one round had struck Smith, the bullet slamming into his left side with the force of a sledgehammer, then punching out his back. He'd lost a great deal of blood and lay so still on the stained bedsheets I was afraid he was slipping away. No, that wasn't right. As I sat beside him, checking his bandages, I couldn't shake the feeling that it was not Chaym but King dying right before me, and all because I'd frozen, paralyzed by my own fear, when I saw the old man draw his pistol and pump round after round into the car. If he died, it was my doing.

Once or twice I thought he'd stopped breathing. Then, just as I was about to run from the room to wake Amy, wind lifted his chest again and clouded the mirror I held close to his mouth. Still, he did not answer when I whispered his name; he remained as remote and unreachable as my mother had been when she was dying in a hospital bed at Cook County and I stayed beside her cooling body night and day, holding her left hand, listening to her breaths come at ever slower intervals. I'd prayed. Bent over her, gripping her hand, I begged the god she'd given me when I was a child to return to me whole the only person in this world who'd cared if I lived or died, but He did not accept the offering of my tears, and she was taken from me, I was orphaned, and whatever flame of faith she'd nurtured in me flimmered out forever. Though I owed Smith my life, I could rekindle none of that. My prayers rang empty in my own ears. Hollow rinds. Form without feeling. And in this fallen condition I could neither pray for his recovery nor believe, if he died, that any part of his personality—his consciousness, his well-stocked mind—would survive the promised failure of the flesh.

Later that night, I walked unshaven, aching in every fiber, into the kitchen, tasting the film on my teeth, so tired I felt even Lena Horne couldn't keep me awake. My eyes ached. I found Amy seated at the table, her lips compressed, toying with something she'd fished from the littered front room. I sat down across from her, picking up the object she pushed toward me. A broken flower vase. Turning it over, I felt my heart tighten. Taped inside was a tiny monitoring device no bigger than a thumbnail.

"I disabled it," said Amy. "Matthew . . . we need to talk. I thought I was strong, but . . . I'm just not cut out to be in the trenches."

"You *are* strong."

"No way." She leaned her head left, the way she did when thinking. "I've never seen anyone shot before. Oh, on TV, sure. Or at the movies. But the real thing? I don't want to see that again. I can't handle it. If you or he had died . . ." She waved away the thought. "I know we're being watched. Maybe right now. And I can't take that. After Chaym is on his feet, I'm going back to the city. You two can stay here. I'll talk to Mama Pearl about it."

"Any chance I can change your mind?"

"None. I'm sorry."

"Suppose Doc calls us? Can you stick it out until the first of the year?"

"Maybe . . . No promises. I want to get on with my life."

My tongue, that traitor, flew ahead of my thoughts. "I'll miss you."

"I think I'll miss you too." All at once, her eyes crinkled and she laughed for the first time in days in that light, effervescent way I'd loved from the first day I met her at school. With her forefinger Amy pushed her glasses back up the bridge of her nose, and looked at me as if for the first time. "I didn't know you very well when we started this. Mama Pearl used to always tell me not to judge a book by its cover. I guess that's really true for bookworms, eh? I mean, Matthew, you talk like a damned thesaurus. You don't think like anybody I know. At first I didn't know what to make of that. Now I know that's just you. And I know something else too. If I was ever in trouble, I'd want you around. Maybe if you get back to Chicago, you could give me a call."

"Amy," I said, "I understand how you feel. What happened last night, with that lunatic we picked up, and the way this place was broken into since we left is . . . *Call you, did you say?*"

"Yes. Call me."

"I . . . I will."

"Oh, but Matthew—"

"What?"

"Get rid of the pencil-holder in your shirt pocket, okay?"

Yet Smith's recovery was not all that concerned us. Upstate in Chicago, where the marches continued, King's high-stakes chess game against that Belshazzar, Daley, grew more daring and dangerous, culminating in a promise to lead his legions into Chicago's no-man's-land for the Negro: Cicero. Richard Ogilvie, the Cook County sheriff, rightly called this "suicide"; he begged the minister to reconsider, but the possibility for bringing to the surface the real face of urban racism for all to see was too great for King to pass up. Not now. Not after Daley'd maneuvered through the courts and Judge Cornelius Harrington to limit the frequency, size, and duration of the demonstrations. And besides, this was the sort of fight his militant detractors were spoiling for—going head-up against the American Nazi Party's George Lincoln Rockwell and every other fascist faction that flew to Chicago to join forces with enraged whites in ethnic enclaves. As the day, August 28, for the assault on Cicero approached, swords were gleefully drawn on both sides.

Then, just two days before C-Day, the mayor blinked, calling for a meeting in the Monroe Room of the Palmer House, where with King he presided over a conference that in effect conceded that his city had not done enough. The meeting lasted ten hours. It included members of the Chicago Real Estate Board, the Housing Authority, and the SCLC, other black activists, Archbishop John Cody, and business leaders. Promises were made to promote fair housing practices and enforce them, encourage legislation, and make colorblind bank loans to qualified families. The Summit Agreement, though not wholly satisfactory to King (it had no guarantees, no schedule, nothing but good intentions), was nonetheless broader in boons won for the black poor than anything he'd achieved in the South, and so he delayed the march into Cicero. Later, at a church on the West Side, he admitted, "Morally, we ought to have what we say in the slogan, Freedom Now. But it doesn't all come now. That's a sad fact of life you will have to live with."

Some, like members of SNCC and Robert Lucas of CORE, refused to live with that. They couldn't wait, they said. To their eyes, the Summit Agreement was a sellout, an emergency exit King used to parachute out of his promise to end slum dwelling in Chicago. Many proclaimed they were tired of being led by middle-class Negroes and rejected the Agreement terms. A new black cat was on the scene, they said, represented by the fierce black masculinity of Stokely, who told it like it was—and by ex-cons in the Black Panther Party. Without King's endorsement, CORE plunged two hundred strong into Cicero in early September, protected by a couple of thousand National Guardsmen. The violence rivaled that of the Marquette march, forcing the marchers to fall back to Lawndale.

After issuing a warning that if the Agreement was not implemented he would renew his agitation, the minister ended his campaign in Chicago and returned to Atlanta, leaving the struggle in Chicago to local groups and Operation Breadbasket, but there was fallout from this northern battle that would follow him forever. After he returned to Atlanta, I phoned him in late October, calling from the same filling station booth I'd used before, and briefly put Smith on the line with him. Although there was depression and lassitude in his tone, the minister thanked Smith and said he would pray for him to soon be back on his feet. The monthly payments would keep coming; when he needed a stand-in, he would be in touch.

But King did not call again, and this was good, because Smith's healing was not quite as we'd expected, or hoped for. In fact, it more resembled a being's slow emergence from a chrysalis than convalescence. And it took months, demanding that Amy stay longer than she'd planned, for the nearness of death had altered him. Indeed, he might *have* died on us a time or two and, like Lazarus, returned to life in a country where the customs and language were only faintly remembered.

He was wan, hollow-eyed, and kept saying, "Gu-od damn, I'm *still* here?" During his convalescence he never quite seemed to get over his astonishment that he was alive. Like so many who've recovered from sickness or injury, he took longer to accomplish ordinary things, having to adjust whatever he did to accommodate his heavily bandaged left side, to relearn how best to stand, lower himself into a chair, and bend forward if he dropped something. Once, I came into his bedroom, carrying a tray with toast, marmalade, and coffee, and I found him propped up on his pillows, lifting his hands to hold shafts of morning sunlight spilling across the air onto his blankets, trying to close his fingers round the bright columns as a child might, then laughing out loud when he failed. He did not want to talk about the attempted assassination he'd foiled, or to claim bragging rights from it. Which baffled me. Wasn't this what he'd wanted? His bid for a place in the history books? In point of fact, Smith spoke very little to Amy and me as he healed. Colors changed in southern Illinois, the days lost their heat, and wind shirred withered leaves and wuthered in the bare treetops. The night air smelled of rain. Around the Nest, he willingly helped us put Mama Pearl's house back in order, and carried water from the well as if doing so simple a task was itself miraculous. He withdrew to his bedroom at night and spent his evenings on a closer study of the minister's sermons, the Pentateuch, Saint Catherine of Genoa, Emerson, the medieval schoolmen, Lotus Sutra, Albertus Magnus, the Vedas (Rig, Sama, Yajur, Atharva), and diverse mystical traditions that piqued his curiosity. (Some evenings I whiffed from behind Smith's closed door the sweet scent of marijuana, and heard the deep-throated, lonely sound, the soul, of his saxophone as it transmuted his anguish and exile into something more vatic than his own weaker voice could convey.) He took notes for himself on the margins of newspapers, hardly noticing the news stories (the defection of Stalin's daughter, riots in more than one hundred American cities), wasting not a single scrap of paper, and in virtually everything to which he turned his hand during his recovery I felt a deepening quiet in him, a turning of his attention away from the social crises and catastrophes we heard broadcast on the kitchen radio (antiwar demonstrations at the Pentagon, Stokely Carmichael's visit to Cuba) to little things—everyday things that had no scribe—with complete absorption and care. To a degree, he seemed more indifferent to himself after the shooting, emptied of envy, as if he lacked the energy to invest in it. For example, Smith simply forgot to shave, letting his mustache evolve into a scraggly goatee that grew into a gray-flecked beard, and his uncombed hair to emerge by inches into an Afro, which diminished by more than a little his striking likeness to King.

Thus, Smith drew not a single stare or whispered comment the Sunday morning we drove Amy to the old Illinois Central train station in the center of Carbondale. On racks near the ticket window there were day-old *Southern Illinoisan* newspapers headlining Muhammad Ali's problems with the draft and the shooting of H. Rap Brown in Cambridge, Maryland, and next to them were displays for candy, Doublemint chewing gum, and sunglasses. Smith purchased a pair (and also some gum), and once he wrapped the glasses round his ears all comparisons to King vanished. One traveler, a young black student from the college, kept staring our way, then tentatively approached where we sat on hard wooden benches waiting for Amy's train, and asked, "Excuse me, sir, are you LeRoi Jones?"

And then the whistle of the Chicago-bound train blew, Amy climbed on board, and within minutes she was waving to us from her window seat as her coach pulled away, taking my heart with it. I stood on the raised cement platform, my trouser legs rippling in wind from the Illinois Central. I waited, wanting her to know I would not leave until the last speck of her coach disappeared in the distance. I took the pencil-holder from my shirt pocket and tossed it away, onto the tracks, and followed a brooding Smith back to the small, crowded parking lot. In silence, we retraced our route through Giant City, came to the road leading to the farmhouse, and Smith, poking a stick of gum between his lips, noticed a few automobiles parked near the Methodist church we'd passed, oh, what must have been a dozen times.

"Pull in there, Bishop. I need to see something."

The church, Bethel AME, sat about fifteen yards back from the road. The rear was under construction—perpetually, I thought, because its congregation, very poor, ran out of money before the framing of much needed additional rooms was finished. For two years, Amy'd told me, Bethel's remodeling had been on hold. Out back, where generations of Griffiths were buried, waist-high weeds obscured the headstones. Its parishioners were plain, country people, primarily elderly women who worked as domestics in white homes in the area, a few retired men living on their pensions, and small children dragged to services by their grandparents. It was not an activist church. Its ranks of teenagers and those in their twenties thinned after the rise of the Black Power movement. They never returned, despite the church's hiring of a young minister from East St. Louis, Rev. Allan Littlewood, to attract them.

From the gravel parking lot, we heard a spirited singing of "Peace Like a River." Smith eased out of the car, holding his left side and listening, his head tilted to the right, humming along, yet he seemed hesitant to move any closer. Next came "Rock of Ages," and as this song shook the walls of Bethel, I took Smith's arm and opened the door, and we slipped inside, treading softly on our soles like thieves, then sat in the last row of seats, hoping not to be seen. There were no more than fifty people in the room. Older women in simple, bright summer dresses held their hymnbooks, fanning with folded copies of the church's newsletter, "The Trumpet." Smith kept on chewing, his eyes tracking left, right, both hands squeezing his knees. He did not look comfortable. But there was something—I couldn't say what—that had drawn him here.

Up front, Rev. Littlewood swabbed his forehead with a wadded handkerchief. He was a thirtyish, dark-skinned man. Jet black in complexion. He wore brown wing tips and unfashionable, heavy-framed black glasses, the sturdy, hard plastic sort you find sold at Army bases. The body he wore, and traveled about in, was thin, with small, bony wrists, and a voice that sounded seminary-trained, soft and scholarly, so gentle I had to bend forward on my seat when the singing ended and Littlewood walked to the small podium, took a sip of water from a pitcher on the table at his right, then asked his congregation to open the Bibles on the back of each bench and turn to Genesis 4:1–16.

"In this passage," he said, "we find a terrible story about the sons of Adam and Eve. The younger brother's murder, which brought death and guilt into our world, is often said to be a prefiguring in the Old Testament of the greater, far grander sacrifice of an innocent who died for our sins at Calvary. For many people—perhaps some of you here today—there is something disturbing in this tale. How can God be just if He rejected one brother's gifts and exalted the other? The story makes our heavenly Father seem as capricious as any creature conjured from dust and condemned to return to dust." Littlewood paused, having lost his place momentarily when he peered up to make eye contact. After finding where he left off, he kept a pencil in his right hand to mark his place when he looked again at the congregation. "I can't believe our Lord is unfair. Remember, it is because He loves the brother who kills that He marks him so no man will do him harm, and it appears none did, for nowhere in the Bible are we told that he dies. And does not God *say* to the elder brother after rejecting his gift that *if thou does well, shalt thou not be accepted*? Long ago, in ancient times, the elder brother's name was interpreted to mean 'possession,' and I believe his sacrifice was intended not to honor the Creator but to glorify himself, to win the Lord's favor like a trophy, or an ornament he might wear. You see, he was given, if not a key to the kingdom, then at least one provocative clue. Oh, a cryptic one, to be sure, but we cannot say that in his moment of dejection he lacked good counsel. His deliverance—and surely ours—is wrapped in the perennial mystery of what that divine counsel, *doing well,* possibly means. Is there a single answer? I think not. As a question, it is open-ended, admitting of only provisional answers, a riddle that yields an inexhaustible reply, which is cast best not as a clever sentence but rather in the quality of sacrifice and sentience itself."

Smith squinted all through Littlewood's sermon, the look on his face skeptical, and he coughed when he heard something questionable. He took out his gum and stuck the wad on the bottom of his seat. I could not tell what he was thinking, though I would have wagered he'd forgotten more about Scripture and the world's spiritual traditions than the young Rev. Littlewood ever knew. After the sermon, Bethel's pastor asked for contributions to help with the church's remodeling. A silver plate was passed around. Then the congregation sang once more—"O Grant Us Light"—and the day's service ended, and a tired Rev. Littlewood positioned himself outside the entrance to shake hands with his tiny flock as they left, ask about their health and their children, and tease the little ones, each of whom he gave a candy cane wrapped in plastic.

When Smith and I reached the door, he said, "I noticed you two gentlemen when you arrived. Thank you for coming. I certainly hope you'll come again. Were you thinking of joining, Mr. . . . uh . . ."

"Chaym Smith. No, I didn't come to join anything."

"Do you live around here?"

"For the time being. It's temporary, like everything."

"Are you a Christian, Mr. Smith?"

Smith chuckled. "You want the truth?"

"Yes, always."

"Well, the truth is, I don't know what I am, and I like it that way. Leaves me lots of room to be surprised every day."

"That's too bad. As you can see, it wouldn't hurt if we had a few more people here."

"Looks like you could use a decent gardener too. Whoever you had before didn't know-jack about landscaping or planting the right flowers for this climate. You want some goldenseal and blackberry lilies out front."

Littlewood sighed. "Yes, you're right. I'd do it, except I work at the bank in town. I have to. My salary is . . . nominal. We need someone to finish the work my predecessor, Reverend McCluskey, started on what was to be the library and a schoolroom for the children. And I wish to God we had someone good to keep up the grounds."

"We could do that."

I blurted out, *"We?"*

"The exercise will do you good, Bishop. The last carpenter they had here didn't know the first thing about framing."

"Could you?" Littlewood's eyebrows raised. "I can't tell you what a great help that would be to us. My problem is, we can't afford to pay much."

"I'm probably not worth much. Whatever you give me is fine."

"We *all* have worth," insisted Littlewood. "If you look in Psalms—"

"Pardon me, Reverend, like I said, I can keep this place up. Thing is, you're better off, though, if you save the sermons—and all them explanations—for Sunday morning. Is that a deal?"

Littlewood laughed. "I'm hardly in a position to refuse anyone's help." He thrust out his right hand. "You have a deal, Mr. Smith."

Were it not for my debt to Smith, and my concern for his recovery, I would have protested his shanghaiing me into involuntary servitude at Bethel AME. Every few weeks I would receive a postcard from Amy detailing the new job she found at Operation Breadbasket, and ending *Miss you.* She was all I thought about during the afternoons Smith and I cleared Bethel's small cemetery, and when we pitched in on the weekends to finish the remodeling left undone and restore areas of the church in ill repair. (Yes, he volunteered me for that too.)

Bethel's cemetery was centuries old. A boneyard overgrown with pickerelweed and wildflowers that obscured shovel-shaped headstones and weathered markers that leaned at angles. Names and dates for the dead, I noticed, were all but obliterated. Here and there I could make out epitaphs for Amy's family. We spent the better part of a week ripping out overgrown bushes, moist, matted neckweeds, thistles and brambles, trimming back trees and hauling away barrels of trash. By dusk each day Smith and I worked until we were too tired to stand, with me perspiring so hard you could tell where I'd been standing because there I left a puddle, like some of me had melted away.

I decided this was too much—all this work—regardless of what I owed him for saving my life. In other words, *he* was doing this to work out his own demons, and all that bedeviled me was the distance between me and Amy.

"Chaym," I said one evening. "I'm going back to the city for a while. There're things I need to do there. Do you think you'll be okay?"

He gave me a headshake. "Do what you gotta do, Bishop. One thing I've always believed, you don't *have* to do what anybody else does. Only what *you* have to do. Ain't no two people on this planet got the same fuckin' *dharma*."

While I cannot speak with authority on the esoteric subject of *dharma*, I can tell you that I was on the first Chicago-bound Illinois Central the very next day, sitting almost alone in a big, clanking coach, on a hard, cushionless seat as the endless cornfields whipped by outside the train's unwashed, thick windows. And because Smith always seemed so obsessed with the story of Adam's two sons, I sat reading a book on them, one I'd borrowed from the college in Carbondale, while the train chuffed and rumbled upstate. In very little time I was lost in this volume that showed how Cain's lineage was legion. In the *Beowulf* poem, Grendel's mother was his child. Down through history, the tribe of Cainites was identified, variously, as that of blacks or Jews who, I recalled, were forced to wear a "mark" by the Nazis (the color black, of course, was its own mark). But by the time Lord Byron wrote his three-act play on the world's first murderer and outcast, Cain was beginning to transmogrify from a figure of evil to one of righteous, tragic singularity, and it was Abel—the obedient, unoriginal son—who began to seem flawed and lacking in selfhood. As I read, I trembled, suddenly realizing how ubiquitous Cain, the metaphysical revolutionary, truly was. He was there in so many novels I'd only haphazardly read, from Hesse's *Demian* to Steinbeck's *East of Eden*, from Miguel Unamuno's *Abel Sánchez* to Melville's *Billy Budd*, and in numerous films I'd enjoyed, such as *Shane* (another name for Cain), and *The Time Machine*, where the Morlocks were descendants of Cain and the Eloi were hapless Abelites (read: dinner). Thinking of another classic Western, *The Magnificent Seven*, it struck me that the besieged Mexican farmers in that film were Abelites through and through, and the gunmen—the down-and-out murderers—who volunteered to save them were all homeless Cainites on the run (except for one, the young Mexican gunfighter manqué played by Horst Buchholz, who was fleeing from the sterility and boredom of his Abelite roots, but by the movie's end embraced it for the love of a village woman), with Yul Brynner saying of the farmers in the movie's last line to Steve McQueen, "We lost. We always lose."

Slowly, by the time the train reached Champaign, I began to see—as if a veil had lifted—the tortured shadow of Cain everywhere, within me and without, his many cultural reincarnations parading through my mind like frames projected on a cyclorama. He was the first city-builder. Perhaps the father of science and philosophy. His war was with God, the Father who spurned him. Of the two—him and Abel—only Cain possessed subjectivity. A complex inner life. It was said that Western man himself was Cain, cursed with the burden of restlessness and the endless quest for selfhood. Down through the centuries, his name was spelled differently in different times. *Caym*, *Kaym*, even *Chaym*, were etymological variations on it.

When I got off the train, lugging my backpack, I felt strange, a bit like a rootless wanderer myself as I boarded a crowded city bus that passed near my studio apartment on the South Side. Beside me on an empty seat I found another rider's discarded *Sun-Times* and tried to read a story about Pablo Picasso's design for a fifty-foot sculpture planned for the plaza in front of the new Civic Center, but from the rear of the bus, on the backseat, a group of Brillo-haired black boys began cursing and laughing way too loud for the comfort of other passengers. They were swapping tales about white people, each one trying to top the others on whether Jews, southern crackers (or northern whites), or Asians mistreated blacks the worst. And then, as if to remind me how much I'd lost the rhythms of the city while at the Nest, they began to sing:

> Jingle bells, shotgun shells,
> Freedom all the way,
> Oh what fun it is to blast
> A trooper man away . . .

I had not been in Chicago in months. I *had* forgotten how deeply hatreds ran here. I was out of touch with this big-shouldered, frontierlike city onto which King had futilely tried to graft the transcendent ideals of Gandhi. Although Chicago was nearly fifty percent black, and was first settled by a Haitian black man (Jean-Baptiste Du Sable) who built his cabin on the north bank of the Chicago River in 1772, all the gleaming buildings and skyscrapers I saw as my bus moved through the Loop, all the twenty-story department stores and high-hat restaurants, the smoking factories, stockyards, movie theaters and museums, libraries, playhouses, radio and television stations, amusement parks and stadiums, were owned by *white* people, as if the Negro was hugely in this Second City but hardly of it. Here, he could be deeply in ward politics, yet where was his economic power, the font from which real politics sprang? Back in the city, I began to feel what Smith called the singular Negro emotion. *Envy*. It came upon me, like a cold or a summer flu, when I stepped down from the bus and onto the sidewalk two blocks from the building I'd lived in before the riots, as if I'd fallen or been flung into an already *finished* world, one where people like me would never, ever fit.

At my building on the South Side, I climbed three flights, hoping no one had broken into my place. I walked down the musty hallway past the communal toilet to my studio apartment—one large room attached to a kitchenette—and turned the key in the lock and entered my city-cave. I wanted to call Amy immediately. But when I switched on the light I was staggered by what I saw. The air felt tight, dead. Months had passed since I'd seen this room with its lumpy Salvation Army sofa, a coffee table I'd picked up at a church rummage sale, and bookcases constructed from cinder blocks and planks of wood. We'd left so quickly for southern Illinois when King okayed Smith's training that my studio was exactly as I'd left it. Dishes caked with Chinese takeout were piled in the sink. Roaches scattered along the counter and cabinets. On the floor by my sofa were pamphlets and application forms for Roosevelt and Columbia College, where I'd planned to reapply, if I could only find financial aid. That, I recalled, had pretty much been my life before Smith appeared: shifting constantly between prayer and economic panic, waging a kind of one-man War on Poverty (my own), because for all President Johnson's promises, and all the ink he'd used signing into law the Civil Rights Act (he went through seventy-two pens), I was always broke. I dropped my backpack inside the door, closed it quietly, and fell onto the sofa, realizing that if anyone *had* broken into my place, they would have found precious little worth stealing— nothing, that is, unless they hoped to pawn my five-volume set of the *Summa Theologica*, boxes of notebooks, or my back issues of *Mind*.

Except for books and a closet of threadbare clothing, I owned nothing. (And even this pitiful studio was a Winter Palace compared with many places where blacks lived.) I wondered: if the minister was right in saying we must not think about what we might get but rather what we might give in a relationship, then what in this world could I offer Amy Griffith? How could I serve *her*? Looking around this room, I saw what a poor catch I was. Very unhip. An old fuddy-duddy at (now) age twenty-five when American culture in the mid-'60s was becoming so fluid, so polymorphous you could change your identity—reinvent yourself—as easily as you restyled your hair. It was the first truly *theatrical* decade. A moment when role-playing and how things appeared took primacy over reality (and who, after all, knew what *that* was anymore?). And me? In this world of flux, I was cursed with a shy, Victorian personality, one Smith's powerful presence had begun to change when I fell into his orbit; but away from him, back in Chicago in my dismal room, I felt again like a moon unmoored. As a colored man raised in the 1950s, I'd learned the hard way to guard my emotions, particularly when I was around white people. I was stiff and proper. Formal and guided by religious principles almost everyone around me (except for King) regarded as obsolete. On the dance floor I drew a blank. (What the hell was "The Bop" anyway?) In social situations I was easy to lose. Or shout down. I tried to be polite, as my mother had taught me (and the minister urged us to do), by patiently listening closely to other people and letting them finish their thoughts, no matter how long that might take, but most often they cut me off or interrupted me in midsentence since I was not an imposing presence and I often quoted from literature or philosophy to reinforce my point, so what I usually had to say went unfinished until I reached home and pulled out my journal and, in the privacy of my studio, completed my end of the conversation there. Hadn't Amy once told me that in a movie I'd make a good prop? That together the best we would ever create was *mud*? Slowly it dawned on me that perhaps her postcards of the last few months were not declarations returning the love I felt for her, but simply examples of her kindness, the sort Amy might show to anyone she pitied.

If that was so, how could I call her?

Two weeks passed before I mustered up the courage to pick up the phone. I busied myself with cleaning the refrigerator and stove, filling out college applications, and at last when I could stall no longer, I picked up the phone and dialed her extension at work.

"You're *here*, Matthew?" In the background I heard the voices of other Operation Breadbasket workers. "What about Chaym?"

"He's downstate. I think he'll be okay. Uh, listen . . . I was thinking if you're not busy tonight, maybe we could go out for dinner, then take in a show—"

"No."

"Oh . . ." *I should have known.*

"There's somewhere special I want to go."

"Where?"

"It's a new place I've been hearing about. Some of the people I work with here have been raving about it, but only black people can get inside. Can you pick me up at five when I get off work?"

"Sure. I'll rent a car. But, Amy, where are we *going*?"

"It's on the West Side, not far from where I used to live. I don't know much about it, Matthew, but I think it's called the Black People's Liberation Library."

9

The library was in a poor neighborhood, squeezed between a pool hall and a tavern. To its left was a vacant lot filled with garbage. Children were playing there, knee-deep in refuse the building's residents dumped from their windows. The smell of decay was overpowering, but no less so than the heartrending sight of black and Puerto Rican families crammed into a building that should have been condemned by the Housing Authority decades before. The El ran right behind the building, rattling its windows. On the first floor, in what had once been a storefront, we found the Black People's Liberation Library. When I parked directly in front of its door, it was 6 P.M. There were about fifteen people inside, white and black, examining the ceiling-high shelves of books on the library's back wall. Nothing about this place seemed exceptional, except for its impoverishment.

"It's *supposed* to look unimportant," Amy said. "People at work told me this is just a front. C'mon, we better get inside before they start."

After checking that the rented car's doors were locked, I followed her through the entrance. Just inside the door, a young black woman sat at a folding card table, a black-bound register open before her. We signed our names, as she asked us to do, then mingled in the small room with other visitors examining titles on the shelves. I saw seminal works by W. E. B. Du Bois, Martin Delany, Marcus Garvey, and dozens of other cultural nationalists and Marxist revolution-aries from Africa, the Caribbean, and South America. I noticed several volumes by Yahya Zubena, a prominent local activist who often got his picture in black publications like the *Daily Defender* and *Jet*. I'd never seen him, but I knew his story. His real name was Willard Bailey, and he was sen-tenced to twenty years downstate in Marion Penitentiary for murdering a nineteen-year-old black filling-station attendant during a stickup (Willard had cut off the boy's genitals and stuffed them in his mouth). But that was only the crime he was convicted for. There were others, ones he wrote about after his release from prison—rape, *dozens* of rapes on the South Side, with some of his victims being only twelve years old. After them, he moved on to assaulting white women on the North Side. In prison, Willard discovered the pleasures of poetry in a creative writing class, as well as the very texts I'd seen by Du Bois and Garvey. According to his interviews and published essays, he was reborn after those experiences, "baptized in blackness," as he was fond of saying. He apolo-gized for his crimes in scathing liberation verse that flowed from his prison cell to periodicals like *Ramparts*. There, a few prominent white authors who published on those same pages declared him too brilliant to be behind bars; they agi-tated for Yahya's release, and by 1967 he was back on the streets of Chicago, reading agitprop poetry in Lincoln Park ("Nigger, Nigger, Wake Up!" was his best-known piece), and some said he was organizing street gangs for the Revolution. Amy pulled down one of Yahya's books and, after pushing her eyeglasses back up her nose with two fingers, began flipping through its pages and frowning. Truth to tell, I found his work puerile, and while I pretended to peruse a copy of *The Souls of Black Folks*, which I deeply respected, I was actually watching Amy from the corner of my eye, wondering if I'd completely blown my first evening out with her.

Half an hour earlier, I'd picked her up outside the office for Operation Breadbasket. She stepped from the building in a group of chattering black women, but I singled her out instantly—my heart trembled ever so slightly, picking up speed—as did other black men on the street, for Amy, with her bee-stung lips and eyes full of laughter, was so striking that it wasn't uncommon for brothers to drive their cars right up on the curb to hit on her. She was wearing a simple, belt-less blue dress that clung nicely to all her corners and, smiling, handed me a map scrawled on office stationery. I was, of course, tongue-tied during the thirty-minute drive to the library, and just listened as she described her new job, her co-workers, and how enticingly they'd talked about the Liberation Library. To be honest, I'd hoped for a kiss when she got in the car, a chaste peck on the cheek, a hug, or *some-thing*. Try as I might, I was unable to read her feelings about me. Nor was I reading myself very well that afternoon (*We always lose*), all of which made me gloomy as I guided the car through rush-hour traffic. There was so much I wanted to say, but I left my thoughts unvoiced, despite my feeling that Amy was always watching me, waiting for me to disappoint her in one of the dozens of ways brothers she'd dated had done before; I always felt she was testing me, and even though we were alone in my car I sensed a chorus line of her erstwhile boyfriends at my elbow, all those black men who'd failed at being faithful, strong, committed to her, aware of her needs; and with my every action I sensed, rightly or wrongly, that I was guilty of their mistakes until I proved otherwise. Only a black American woman could place that burden on a man. Yet it wasn't simply about her. Or me. No, it was all that painful history behind us, the centuries of black men and women hurting and betraying and possibly hating each other since the days of slavery when a Negro risked death if he defended his family; the damage wrought by centuries of discrimination was always there, right at the heart of something as private as passion, despite pleas for forgiveness and promises to forget the past and make a fresh start. It was about my mother Ellesteen's bitterness toward my father, that pathetic bastard, after he took off and left her to raise me alone. Oh yes, all *that* was in the car between us, unspoken and perhaps unspeakable, and I hadn't the faintest idea in such an uncertain world how we could begin.

"Matthew," she said, reeling me back from remembrance, "I think they're starting."

White visitors drifted outside, obviously bored by the Liberation Library's familiar titles. Once the last white person stepped to the street, the young woman at the table stood up and latched the door, locking in the eight blacks who remained. She walked to a section of the bookshelves, reached behind a row of works by Chester Himes—I heard a click—and that section of the shelf swung open into the outer room, as grandfather clocks do in old British movies set in haunted houses. I made an in-suck of breath, as startled as the other black visitors, for behind the tiny room in which we'd waited, there was a larger space, with huge colored maps of every major city in America on the walls, and five rows of folding chairs before a podium.

Yahya Zubena welcomed us inside.

"Matthew," Amy whispered, "this isn't what I expected at all. Isn't he supposed to be in jail?"

"I read in *Jet* that he got out last year."

"No one at work told me this was his library."

Her reaction to him was visceral, the recoil any woman might feel in the presence of a man who, after his prison conversion, confessed in his books that he raped blacks as "practice," as a warm-up to perfect his technique for whites in the suburbs. But we couldn't leave. We were locked inside. I had to nudge Amy between her shoulder blades to coax her into entering the back room, but I was so dazed myself I don't exactly remember walking in, only that Yahya said, "Now that the ofays are gone, we can get down to business." He ordered us to follow him to a map of Chicago at our left. By any measure, he was a big man—linebacker big—with a Farmer Burns build, full-bearded, and a complexion one shade up from sepia. He wore faded jeans, work boots, and a dashiki of red, black, and green, the colors of Marcus Garvey's flag. As large as he was, Yahya made the back room's sparse furnishings feel as flimsy as constructions of pasteboard and papier-mâché. In a word, he was one of the darlings of the white media, one of King's competitors for press coverage, and every parole officer's worst nightmare.

"Brothers and sisters," intoned Yahya, "I want y'all to look at that map and tell me whereabouts you live."

We all did so, indicating addresses in south and west Chicago. That pleased Yahya. He steered our group toward the map of Detroit. "If y'all got relatives there, show me where they live." A few people pointed toward the heavily industrial portions of the city. Again Yahya smiled. He moved us on from map to map, from Oakland to Harlem, Cleveland to Philadelphia, and each time he asked, "Where do most black people live?" The answer unfailingly was in some urban district near factories and commerce.

"Now, I want y'all to sit down and listen carefully." He waited until we were all seated on the folding chairs. "I took you through those maps because I wanted you to see for yourself that it ain't no accident where we live forms a *pattern*. A concentration camp. We're always near highways or factories or warehouses or railroad tracks. Ain't that so? You might say we're *contained*. We're concentrated in the areas where the Man wants us—*away* from him. Segregation did that, but from a strategic standpoint it did something else. What you think that *is*?" Fingers in his beard, he paced, sometimes pausing to stand directly over visitors in the front row where Amy and I sat, looming over us with his face only inches from ours. "I'ma tell you. Being concentrated like that means when y'all start rebelling against your miserable conditions, tearing up the city like you did a year ago, all Charlie's got to do is move his tanks and trucks and National Guard troops right down the freeways and Illinois Central tracks to your front door."

"Excuse me." I cleared my throat. "What about blacks who don't live there? Aren't we a little more dispersed than these maps show?"

"I don't *think* so, brother. Maybe you better look again, or clean them Coke-bottle glasses of yours."

A couple behind Amy and me chuckled. The skin on my face tingled. "I was just asking if—"

Yahya scowled me into silence.

There was a pleat between Amy's brows. "Why are you telling us this?"

"So you can *prepare*, sistuh."

"For what?"

Yahya stepped toward her, so close we could smell him; he forced her to look up at him. I felt Amy stiffen. She placed her right hand on top of mine. "Why you think, girl? For the coming race war."

"I don't believe there *is* one coming, not if people of goodwill, white and black, do everything they can to make things better. Until a little while ago, I worked with Dr. King. Right now I work at Operation Breadbasket—"

Yahya grinned. "For King, huh? I guess we got some Uncle Tom nigguhs here. When the Revolution comes, y'all got to *go*."

Now Amy was trembling. "You'd kill other black people?"

"Sistuh, I hate to say this, but you'n and that brother sound like house niggers to me. I don't think you understand anything about the necessity of revolutionary violence. I'd appreciate it if you'd let me finish talking to the *real* black people in this room."

Amy squeezed my hand so tightly I feared she might break the bones in my fingers. Witheringly, she gave me a sad, sideways look, as if to say, *I'm sorry, I didn't know.* I leaned back on my chair, wanting to leave but knowing we were Yahya Zubena's captives until he finished. Against my will, I listened while he instructed the others on what to do when the white man came to get them, as Nazis had rounded up Jews in Poland thirty years before. Come they would, said Yahya. It was only a matter of time because blacks were asking for too much too quickly. "I'm telling y'all, the white man would rather blow it all up rather than give it up!" The evidence for this, he explained, was in the history books, where any fool could see that Caucasians were driven to conquest and oppression because they were "ice people" who came from cold European climates and subjugated ancient, peace-loving "sun people" everywhere in Africa. (Was I imagining this, or hadn't the minister once said, "The Negro knows nothing of Africa, he is an American"?) He droned on and on, his descriptions of whites as Cainites and coloreds as Abelites fascinating to me, given the book I'd read on the train, and I thought of Chaym as he outlined his airtight, one-dimensional interpretation of history, one in which there was no room for ambiguity, or for counterexamples to his arguments, or for people like John Brown, Frederick Douglass, or even Jackie Robinson. His historical vision was *kitsch*. Revolutionary *kitsch*. The way he reasoned, with racial politics as every syllogism's major premise, led all his thoughts to the same terminus. (Of course, if the only tool you have is a hammer, it's likely you'll treat every problem—and person—as a nail.) I doubted his comparison of black communities to concentration camps, and his claim that Negroes could never be racist because, as Yahya said, "You can't be racist unless you have power. Black folks don't have power, so we can't be racist." It was the logic of Humpty Dumpty, who told Alice, "When *I* use a word, it means just what I choose it to mean—neither more nor less," and there in the Black People's Liberation Library, I felt as if I'd fallen down a rabbit hole into a Wonderland where all the world's meanings were reversed. Yahya reminded me of the militant black students I met at Columbia College, dashiki-wearing radicals who, after I'd contradicted one of them at a meeting of the Black Student Union, told me I wasn't black enough to belong to their group. They cast me out of their meetings. In response, I formed, then briefly led, the first Bible study group on campus for a year before my faith in the god of the Book began to fade. They (and Yahya) made me recall King, who warned, "There are some who are color-consumed and they see a kind of mystique in being colored and anything noncolored is condemned." And even more importantly, "We shall have to create leaders who embody virtues we can respect."

By the time Yahya finished, Amy looked ill. Noticing this, Yahya cut his eyes our way. "I don't suppose *you* two agree with me, do you?"

Her words were hardly above a hiss. "I've seen good white people who sacrificed their lives on Freedom Rides.

Andrew Goodman and Michael Schwerner were killed and buried under a Mississippi dam right beside James Chaney."

"Uh-hunh, I heard about that. It's sad, sistuh, but the way I see it, your average white boy won't go that far. Some of 'em might fight for colored folks when they're young and rebelling against their elders, but sooner or later they get that wake-up call from their own people, who pull their coat to the fact that it's their privileged future they're foolin' with, and if they keep acting up, they won't be on top no more. What *that* means is they gonna cut their hair, clean themselves up, and put on a three-piece suit with a pair of red suspenders, and shake off the woolly-headed woogies they been hanging out with. Naw, honey, white boys *always* make sure they got it better than us."

"And you believe that?" she asked. "Are you saying Dr. King's life is poorer—as a life—than Richard Speck's?"

"Speck's white, ain't he?"

With that, Amy stood up. "Can we *leave* now, please?"

"Maybe you'd better," said Yahya.

Back in the car, she was too exasperated to speak as we pulled away. Finally she brought out, "I'm *sorry*, Matthew! I would never have taken you there if I'd known what it was about."

"You don't have to apologize—"

"Yes, I *do*! I suppose when *he* takes over, he'll drive people like you and me into the gas chambers. Mama Pearl always told me that *any*body who tried to get me to hate was my enemy." Leaning back on the seat, she took a long breath. Then, unexpectedly, she laughed. "I've *dated* guys who talked like him. Can you believe that? They're the reason I wasn't seeing *any*body when we met. I mean, I'd given up. All that hate for the white man turned *so* quickly—if I disagreed with them—into some of them slapping me hard enough to shake loose my teeth. Or they'd use that excuse about the Man holding them down as the reason why they couldn't keep a job and expected *me* to support them—and their drug habits! I was just sick of it, that's all." Amy paused, looking me up and down as I pulled to a stop at an intersection. "There's no hate in you, Matthew. I like that. *I trust* that. And I'm glad you got rid of that silly pencil-holder."

"Do . . . do you want to get something to eat?"

"No, I'm not hungry. Just take me home, okay?"

She'd found a new apartment, this one located on the corner of Dearborn and Huron. After I parked, Amy asked, "Would you like to come up for a drink or something?" I said yes. (I was less interested in the drink than in the "something.") I followed her up one flight to a door it took her forever to unlock (there were four padlocks and latches on it). Once inside, I saw that sixty dollars a month bought her an efficiency apartment divided into a living room, a kitchen, and a minuscule bath. Her front room was furnished ceiling to floor with bookshelves (I noticed titles I'd given her by Jean Toomer and Claude McKay when we were in college, ones in which I'd playfully signed the authors' names and written glowing praise for her), and tables and chairs made from driftwood. The floors were bare. A fisherman's net swung from the ceiling. On the wall over her sofabed were black-and-white movie (*Stormy Weather*) and theater (*A Raisin in the Sun*) posters. Amy tossed her purse onto a chair, flipped through her album collection quickly, and put John Coltrane's *A Love Supreme* on her stereo. On the kitchen counter she lit a stick of pine incense; then she popped open the refrigerator and filled two wineglasses with pinot noir.

Twilight was coming on, thickening throughout her rooms, spreading inside the apartment like a tone, a touch of the keys on the far left side of a piano, like a stain of teal-blue watercolor that caught along the surface of the wineglass she handed me and reflected off her windows. A whiff of twilight even tinctured shadows in the corners: a base color lying beneath all others as streetlights below us on Dearborn winked on and night's density gathered in her curtains and—yes—in my mind, because I couldn't believe I was standing there, sipping wine that flew right to my head, and Amy was kicking off her shoes and looking at me in the way I'd imagined only in my dreams.

"After tonight I feel . . . soiled. I think I need to take a shower."

"Oh . . ." I stammered. "Go ahead, I'll wait out here."

"I was hoping, Matthew, you'd take it *with* me."

Straightaway, she disrobed, leaving her blue dress and white undergarments on the floor, and walked—I want to say *floated*—toward her bathroom. Believing I was dead or dreaming, I pinched my arm. Ouch. Then I heard water spurting a room away. I shed my own clothes as quickly as I could, hurried barefoot to the bathroom, and found Amy soaping her shoulders in billowing clouds of steam. I squeezed into the small cubicle with her. Instantly my glasses began to fog. Very gently she lifted them off my face, pressed her lips against mine, then handed me the bar of Lifebuoy. With it I lathered my hands, and as she closed her eyes, lifting her head a little, my fingers traced her forehead and cheeks, then moved down, soaping every crevice and swale, and it was as if I was sculpting her the way Pygmalion did his masterpiece, slowly discovering every muscle and fold, as I massaged from Amy's chin to her calves, and then she did the same for me, lathering places where I didn't know I even had places, and then we toweled each other dry, both of us a little drunk by then from touching and pinot noir, and dropped onto her bed, and I said, *Tell me what you want me to do,* which she did, and for the next two hours—or perhaps it was three—I did everything Amy wanted, in just the way she wanted it, for I *do* pride myself on my work, whatever it is.

"Well," she said when we were done, "I guess it's true."

I was groggy, squinting at her electric alarm clock: 11:30. "What's true?"

"Still waters run deep."

I was trying to figure out what she meant by that when the telephone on a table beside her bed rang. Amy picked it up, pressed it against her ear, and said, " 'Lo?" As she listened, her face changed. She said, "Chaym, is that *you*?" Moments later the phone was dead. Amy placed it back on its base, her expression that of bewilderment.

"Matthew . . . something's wrong."

"That was Chaym? How did he get your number?"

"The same way you did. The phone book. He must have called me from that filling station in town—"

"What did he *say*?"

She swung her feet over the side of the bed, pulled on an old housecoat, and sat away from me on a chair, squeezing her hands, her knees pressed together. "I don't *know* what he was talking about! Something about . . . a green Plymouth, people watching him. Did you see a car like that?"

I had, but I said nothing.

"I'm worried. I think you should see if he's okay."

"*Now*?"

"Yes, now!" she said. "We made Dr. King a promise."

"That's a six-hour drive! We were just beginning to—"

"I'll *be* here when you get back. Do you love me?"

"How can you even ask?"

She stepped back to the bed. I lifted my left arm, and she slid in close, her head on my shoulder and her hand on my chest. "Then you'll do it for me, right?" Leaving her was the last thing I wanted to do, and at that moment I hated Smith. But being me, I remembered words I'd taped long ago on my

178

refrigerator door: *Love feels no burden, thinks nothing of trouble, attempts what is above its strength, pleads no excuse of impossibility; for it thinks all things lawful for itself and all things possible. It is therefore able to undertake all things, and it completes many things, and warrants them to take effect, where he who does not love, would faint and lie down.* Thomas à Kempis. Of course, *he* was never asked to leave the bed of a woman who looked better than a batch of Miss Gurdey Maye's buttermilk biscuits.

The sacrifices I made for the Movement . . .

"Matthew?"

"Okay, I'm *going.*"

By late afternoon, I was back in Makanda, cursing Smith as I climbed the steps to the farmhouse. He was nowhere to be seen, so I drove to Rev. Littlewood's church, wondering if something evil had befallen him, which is what I'd deliciously imagined during the long drive, but now I was worried and feeling guilty that I'd left him when so many people wanted King dead and might mistake Smith for the minister. It was a Friday. The church was vacant. I used one of the keys Rev. Littlewood had given us when we started work on Bethel to let myself in. I looked to no avail for Smith but noticed something else. Portions of the church dated from different periods, like a palimpsest, reaching back to the end of the Civil War when black couples separated by slavery held mass weddings on this very site, as many as a hundred men and women gathering to exchange wedding vows and have their long-deferred unions sanctified and cemented by the Christian faith.

The structure was a tissue, a layering of lives and architectural styles based not on the principle of either/or but of adding this to that, and yes of course throw that in too, the Jewish, the Christian, the Greek, the African, the Roman, the English, the Yankee, for these could only enrich the experience of the spirit. On either side of the entrance were two cracked stained-glass windows of intersecting tracery, the mullions of each branching out into curved bars, below them smooth masonry with chamfered edges. Under the direction of the church's first pastor, the congregation finished the church's foyer and stairs leading up to the sanctuary, but it fell to the next generation to complete the choir stand and the storeroom where wooden crates containing the church's archives—tithings, mimeograph copies of a weekly newsletter, and records on christenings, funerals, and donations—were stacked almost to the ceiling; then it fell to a third generation to raise additional rooms in the rear for special meetings. In the original braces strengthening the frame of the roof, in the quoins at the church's four corners, in the small choir section to the left of the pulpit, added during the 1920s by parishioners whose names were now lost, I saw a creation that on every level—from purlins to wallplates—transcended the passing of its founders, one that no single generation could live to see completed and thus was handed down and on to those yet unborn for its continual restoration and completion.

From this ground of blended anonymous lives, many a world-acclaimed king might arise.

Where I fit into this sanctuary so heavy with black history, I could not say. Before returning to Chicago I'd simply fit myself behind a wheelbarrow, hauling away debris as Smith cleaned and polished the pews, doing and redoing the architrave and shutting stile with a painstaking care I found as hard to fathom as his spontaneous act of volunteering first as a caretaker, then helping to finish the additions left undone, and at last, just as I was leaving, offering to teach one of the Sunday-school classes for Rev. Littlewood, explaining Old Testament stories to Bethel's wide-eyed children with the skill that only a natural thespian could bring. He told me he planned to act out the tales, taking the parts of Noah and Job and others; he especially enjoyed the opportunity to play a fickle Jehovah with a cruel streak in Him. I knew—just *knew*—the children would love it. I imagined them cheering during his classes. He even talked about possibly directing the children in biblical plays of their own. But, I wondered, why this sacrifice for a community in which he believed himself an outcast?

The answer and Chaym were waiting for me in the church's storeroom. I found him cleaning up after a day of painting, for which he was miserably paid, scrubbing turpentine-soaked rags on his trousers, shirt, and portions of his face splattered with Optic White. Looking up, he saw me and winked.

I asked, "You like what you see?"

"Hey now, that's *my* line, Bishop. You get your own. But, yeah, I do like what I see. That big Cheshire cat grin means you musta got some trim in Chicago. That's good. Keep at it, and those pimples on your face might clear up."

"Watch how you talk about Amy. I was there when you called her. The only reason I'm back here so soon is because *she* was worried about you."

"About *me*? Worried, eh?"

"Yes, I know it sounds strange—"

"Hell, I'm all right. I just got my hands on a li'l gorilla dust last night and thought I saw somethin' outside. Wasn't nobody there when I looked again. But I'm straight today, and I *am* glad to see your ass. You can help me move some of these paint cans upstairs."

"Uh-uh, *no*! I've done enough work here, and I don't know why you're doing it. Did you get religion or something after you got shot?"

"Naw, Bishop," he said as he leaned back, resting his

arms on the bench. "I don't believe in a blessed thing, including me. I'll never be one of the faithful. It's just that I figure work is all I got to offer, even if the ground we till gives back nothing. It don't matter. I ain't worried 'bout it bein' fair. For a li'l while what I do here is just what I'm doin' and, who knows, it may be beautiful, and maybe nobody won't know 'bout it, even God, but for a second or two it'll make a few of the folks who come through here on Sunday happy. I don't 'spect much more'n that anymore." He stared as I rubbed my lower back. "What's the matter? You feel stiff?"

"Some. I just drove for over six hours. Remember?"

"Got just the thing for you. Come with me."

Smith led me from the storeroom to the platform on which Rev. Littlewood's pulpit sat. He pushed it back to widen the space where we stood, then spread his feet shoulder width. Closed his eyes. Tucked in his tail, slowly raised his arms chest high, and said, "Do like I'm doing. Keep it slow. Don't stop. Just flow."

"I've seen this on TV. All those Chinese you see in the park every morning in Peking do this, right?"

"Wrong." He kept moving, flowing through postures, his weight never equally distributed on both feet. "What they're doing is a lie, like most things. The Communists under Mao have outlawed all the old, traditional martial arts 'cause they can't control them, or the genius of those venerable old kung fu masters. But people are practicin' in secret anyway. So the government concocted the form you seen on TV so the practitioners would *have* to do it out in the open at the parks—where the government can watch the herd and take names—since *that* form requires lots of room. What I'm showing you is the real thing done by monks at the Shaolin monastery. You can do it in a shower stall if you adjust your footwork. It don't take up no more room than that. When you do it, do it *riabroi*."

"Huh?"

"Oh, sorry. That's a Thai word. There's no English equivalent. I picked it up in Chiang Mai. It's yours. I'ma give it to you. *Riabroi* means everything together at once, complete, sensible, beautiful, perfect, and natural. You do this form— or anythin' else—*riabroi* and you won't need me lookin' after you no more."

"Looking after *me*? I'm the one Doc told to—"

"Bishop, shut up and do the form."

I followed his lead, letting him teach me the twenty-four moves of the (Yang) Tai Chi Chuan form he'd picked up while traveling overseas, making myself slow down more with each posture, each breath, wasting no motion whatsoever, and as I mimicked his movements I began to feel lighter and less fatigued—like water, like wind—though I'm sure if Rev. Littlewood had entered Bethel AME just then, he would have found it puzzling to see two black men, both refugees of the American race wars, doing Taoist-drenched Tai Chi in the Christian sanctuary where generations of right and proper Griffiths had prayed to a god unknown to either Lao Tzu or Chuang Tzu.

On our way back to the Nest that evening my anger at him for making me leave Amy was, strange to say, replaced by an ineffable peace. "Do that form three times in a row every day," he advised, "and you'll live longer than that colored ex-cowboy in Texas named Charlie Smith I was reading about." His promise of longevity made me laugh, but I agreed to do as he asked, for had he not proven himself to be, despite his crabbiness and infuriating eccentricities, an experienced guide for those of us, broken-winged, condemned to mediocrity and the margins of the world? All during the ride back I felt this fraternity with him, but I had no idea I was not alone in my admiration.

As I pulled up the road I saw the green Plymouth parked near the farmhouse and two travel-stained men sitting on our porch as if they owned it.

"Watch yourself," said Smith. "Let me handle this."

The older of the two men, gourd-shaped with dull egg-blue eyes behind his thick glasses, his tie tucked under his belt, stood up as we got out of the car and came up the footpath, scratching the side of his head where he needed a shave. He took off his hat. The movement exposed for a second the shoulder holster inside his wrinkled suitcoat and the butt of a snub-nosed .38.

"Evening, Chaym," he said. "We've been waiting for you."

I stayed to one side of Smith, my palms beginning to perspire.

"Evening yourself. You fellahs lost?" Smith's eyes burned into them. "You're pretty far off the main road—"

"No, this is where we want to be. My name is Jasper Groat and"—he made a twitchlike nod—"my colleague there is Vincent Withersby. We—say, do you think we could talk inside for a little while?"

"Depends on what you want, Mr. Groat."

"Oh." Groat laughed and dipped inside his coat; then his palm displayed a shiny, official-looking badge pinned to his wallet. "That's simple. We want to talk. To offer you a way to make a little money and maybe help your country out during difficult times. That sound good to you? I certainly hope it does. The people we work for are very . . . *interested* . . . in Martin Luther King. Our director thinks your success impersonating King could, um, be . . . useful . . . for one of the projects we've been kicking around the office for a coupla years. Couldn't find the missing piece, though, till you showed up. Damn, you do look like him, you know? Even behind those dark glasses and that beard. You think we might rest a spell inside, put our feet up, and chat awhile?"

To his left, Withersby was packing enough Dunhill tobacco into his Liverpool pipe to last for an hour. Regardless of what we said, they planned to stay. So I slid open the screen door, stepped to one side, and bid them enter.

IO

*On the floor of their living room in Atlanta, with the rugs
rolled back into a corner and furniture pushed to one side, he
was wrestling with his children, pinning Dexter's arms while
Marty, one arm around his neck, rode his back in an effort to
topple him so both boys could get the upper hand. Away to the
left in his workroom the phone rang and rang. His wife looked
on from the hallway, shaking her head. Can't you find somewhere else to play with these kids? The tussle, which had gone
on for ten minutes of giggling and tickling, was the first good
wrestling bout he'd had with the children since they left
Chicago; in fact, it was the first time they'd had his undivided
attention in weeks, so he was hardly about to stop.*

*They were happy to be home again, the wretched flat on
South Hamlin just a horrible memory now, a place that all
summer long drained the gaiety from his children and*

depressed his wife. No, moving them there was what the Move-
ment required at the time, but he swore he would never, God
willing, subject them to that sort of hardship again. If he
regretted anything about his life, it was the way the Cause took
such a devastating toll on his personal life and the roles he
cherished the most, those of father and husband. Every so often
he felt tempted to call his schedule suicide on the installment
plan. The crowds and faces ran together. On so many morn-
ings he awoke in a different hotel in a strange city, and for a
few bewildering moments he sat up in bed wondering where
on earth he might be. And the meals his admirers served him?
How they played hob with his waistline! He remembered one
in particular—the food itself, not the occasion or his hosts.
There was a hundred-year-old bottle from Oporto, lobster on
Canton china as thin as a wafer, frittura mista, *and pale game*
served so ingeniously, so artfully, it looked as though each slice
had been cut from butter. Yet, if the truth be known, he pre-
ferred catfish, pigs' feet, and collard greens. At least at home
now he could relax for a little while and eat whatever he
pleased. And, thank God, he didn't have to shave. Daily use of
the lye-based depilatory powder his sensitive skin required
often left his face tender, smarting and feeling raw, stinging in
the outdoor air. But now that they were back in Atlanta, he
knew his tortured skin would have a few days to heal.

His children were calling, beckoning him back from his
workroom, where he'd finally hurried to answer the phone, to
the living room and the makeshift handball court they'd cre-
ated by pushing back furniture and rolling up the rug. His
work space was on the same floor, a back room where his gray
metal desk was barricaded in by a file cabinet, a confusion of
boxes, shelves loaded down with books, his notes for Where Do
We Go from Here?, *mounds of correspondence, and the*
phone he held burning against his ear. His hands began to
shake as he listened, thinking how when he awoke each morn-

ing he could never know what new catastrophe awaited him, what novel, Job-like species of pain hunkered in the shadows, or what manner of crisis, personal or political, he would be put through next. On the other end, as his Marty and Dexter shouted for him to join in their game, the agent in the Atlanta office was reporting almost gleefully the latest bounty the Bureau learned had been placed on his head.

Usually, he suspected, they didn't call when they discovered someone bent upon killing him. The policy was, he was sure, to simply sit back, wait, and see if the assassin made good on his promise. But this was different. The amount to be collected for killing him was $50,000. "Pretty high, eh?" the agent said. "Bet you didn't know you were worth that much . . ."

Even on his best day he didn't believe himself worth that much. Or the staggering smear campaign Hoover launched in 1964, aimed at exposing him, as the director put it, as "the most notorious liar in the country" and removing him from "the national picture." His agents maintained a two-bedroom apartment in Atlanta's Peach Street Towers filled with surveillance equipment, and kept a man in the place twenty-four hours a day, monitoring every call he made or received. Attorney General Robert Kennedy'd approved the first wiretaps on his home and offices (though not the fourteen microphone surveillances that came later) after his brother, the president, expressed grave concern over the help the SCLC received from Stanley Levison and Hunter Pitts O'Dell. He remembered that conversation well. Kennedy invited him to the White House and during a stroll in the Rose Garden said, "They're Communists, you've got to get rid of them. If they shoot you down, they'll shoot us down too—so we're asking that you be careful." He'd left that meeting convinced that Hoover's office, not Kennedy's, was the center of power in Washington. And that office was determined to see him dead.

Having hung up, having forced himself to say, "Thank you

for the information," he closed his workroom door and slumped onto the chair in front of his desk. Suddenly he felt too tired to play with the children. Too tired to move. The call had washed away all his strength. For an instant he felt dizzy and lowered his head onto a pile of week-old letters begging for his attention. He'd faced death so many times before—the bomb that exploded in Room 30, his room at the Gaston Motel during the Birmingham campaign, flashed through his memories. But this? Oh, this new threat was something else. This plan to kill him had been hatched in Imperial, Missouri, at the home of John Sutherland, who was putting up the money. He was a Virginian, a product of military schools and a descendant of the Pilgrims; he stood firmly against the Movement, so much so that he founded the St. Louis Citizens Council and served in an antiblack organization of businessmen called the Southern States Industrial Council. As the agent told it, Sutherland knew an underworld figure named John Kauffmann, a drug dealer and operator of the Bluff Acres Motel, where stolen cars were dropped off occasionally by nickel-and-dime thugs of his acquaintance. One of them was Russel Byers. His brother-in-law John Paul Spica was serving a murder sentence in the Missouri State Penitentiary, sharing a cell with a penny-ante crook named James Earl Ray. Byers, the agent said, made one of his calls on Kauffmann that fall of 1966, and the motel owner asked him if he'd like to make some money. Sure would, Byers said. Then there's someone, replied Kauffmann, I think you ought to meet.

He drove the car thief to Sutherland's place. The Virginian met them at the door, wearing a Confederate colonel's cap. He invited them into his den, festooned with a rug imprinted with the Stars and Bars and a huge Rebel flag on one wall. There, Sutherland informed them he represented a covert southern group with deep pockets. They would pay $50,000 to anyone who killed the "big nigger" from Atlanta. Was he interested?

Byers listened politely, then said he needed a while to think over the offer. There was little chance he would accept, said the agent—Byers knew danger when he saw it—but in the underworld of Kauffmann, Byers's brother-in-law, and Ray, it was widely known that an open contract had been issued for King's head.

It was, he knew, only a matter of time before someone collected that bounty. Pushing aside the papers on his desk (his aides told him he'd already generated close to 200,000 pages of documents), he found his pack of cigarettes. He pulled one out, searched his pockets for a matchbook, then lit the cigarette, extinguished the match with his thumb and forefinger, and sat back in his chair. How many days did he have left? Or should he be thinking now in terms of hours? Maybe minutes? What should a man do when at any moment he might be struck down?

He knew.

If he might not see tomorrow, then what he wished for most was to receive forgiveness from those he'd failed, beginning with his children. And his wife. Whatever failures there were in their marriage he blamed on himself, for no man could have asked for a better partner to share his life since 1952. She was pursuing her music career—as a singer of exceptional talent—at the New England Conservatory when they met in Boston. Yes, she'd heard of him before they met, and her impressions were not favorable. In Boston he was known for the brilliant sermons he delivered at local churches, but Coretta had reservations about the Baptist ministers she'd met. They were so . . . emotional, and she was hoping to align herself with a less fundamental, more liberal approach to religion. Added to that, the stuffiness of so many Baptist ministers bothered her. And wasn't this M. L. King just a little too popular with the women in town? She'd heard he was brilliant, and had been accepted at Edinburgh University for graduate work (though Yale turned him down); he brought together other students at his place on St. Botolph Street for meetings of what they dubbed "The Dialectical Society," at which they as well as their professors presented papers. She'd also heard he was playful, a good dancer and a party boy, a tease who dressed to the nines—a real ladies' man, by most accounts, and Boston's most eligible young black bachelor. It was with some reservation, then, that she surrendered to the matchmaking of her friend Mary Powell, who was married to the nephew of his former teacher, Benjamin Mays at Morehouse, and ate at the Western Lunch Box, an eatery specializing in down-home cooking, where black students—he among them—gathered to relax and talk. Mary warned him that Coretta might not be religious enough for his temperament, but at that point in his life he was frustrated by the women he was meeting. The woman he hoped to marry, he told Mary, must have four characteristics: character, intelligence, personality, and beauty. Mary, saying nothing, simply gave him Coretta's phone number.

When he picked her up in his green Chevy on the Huntington Avenue side of the conservatory—she with her coat buttoned to her throat and wearing a scarf, thinking of the struggles and sacrifices that had brought her from a culturally deprived background to Antioch and at last to her training here—her first thought when his car pulled up had been, Oh my God, look what a runt he is. (In point of fact, he was 166½ pounds that year, 66¼ inches tall, and had a blood pressure of 134/64.) To her he at first seemed full of the slick, superficial language—the jive—of black men with only one thing on their minds. But no. As they spent time together that afternoon, in the cold rain of a January afternoon, she began to see deeper into his passion for Continental theology and his people's deliverance. He was working that term, he said, in directed study with Professor DeWolf on a paper he would entitle "Karl Barth's Conception of God," and as he discussed his conclusions with her he grew more animated, explaining that Barth's God was too removed from man, wholly Other, which he found unacceptable; but there was much in so-called crisis theology that, in his view, corrected liberal Protestantism's sentimentalization of man. They sat in Sharaf's Restaurant on Massachusetts Avenue, eating a cafeteria-style lunch. He put down his fork and leaned closer toward her, saying, "Maybe man is more a sinner than liberals are willing to admit." In his paper's conclusion he planned to question liberalism's naïve, ivory-tower belief in progress. "Instead of assured progress in wisdom and decency man faces the ever-present possibility of swift relapse not merely to animalism but into such calculated cruelty as no other animal can practice." Talking on, waving his fork then, he watched her closely for her reaction, and was pleased by her attention and her bobbing her head in agreement when he said, "The word sin has to come back into our vocabulary. One hoary meaning of the word is 'to miss the mark,' as when an arrow goes astray. I like that. What do you think?"

"I think you've given it a lot of thought," she said.

Yes, he was far more than she'd expected.

And he could not keep his eyes off her. That day she was wearing bangs with a natural wave. That he liked. Indeed, he liked everything about her, even though he knew he would have to confront Daddy King head-on—a thing he dreaded more than anything else—when he brought this stunning woman, who was not one of Ebenezer's own, home and introduced her as his fiancée. "You," he told her, "are my Waterloo."

No man, he knew, would ever have a better companion by his side. When they were married in Alabama on June 18, 1953, the local Jim Crow laws prohibited them from spending their wedding night in a hotel. Instead they found lodging at a black funeral home. Yes, they had been through much together. As in most traditional, black southern Baptist households, she followed his lead, going so far as to let him tell her how she should dress or when she should fix herself up a little. If these were faults—failures in his understanding of equality—he regretted them, because in those early years of their marriage he felt liberated by her to at last be himself. He owed her that, an intimacy he'd never experienced before, one possible only through the strange alchemy of marriage, where two once separate and distinct histories blended to become a single destiny. True, he learned that this kind of love involved suffering, the extinction of the ego, but the trade-off, especially after the children were born, was his rebirth as a fully communal being, a man working in concert with another for the welfare of his family, which reinforced his passion for politics and social justice. In his later speeches, the ones assailing America's crass and vulgar materialism, he was fond of saying, "The great problem facing modern man is that the means by which we live have outdistanced the spiritual ends for which we live." What he didn't say—and now wondered if he should have—was that through Coretta's love he'd come to know that ecstatic freedom and the fullness of being-with.

He wondered how badly she'd been hurt by the stories about his sexual affairs. There were women all over the country who claimed they'd known his affections. The rumor mill thrived on tales about the Kennedy brothers, or Lyndon Baines Johnson, who, according to a widely circulated and probably false report, unzipped his pants during a White House meeting and dropped his Texas-sized member on the conference table, asking, "Does Ho Chi Minh have one of these?" Because the public loved stories like these about the famous and powerful he was not surprised to hear them said about himself. But did any of his detractors stop once to admit that these stories about his wearing sunglasses and meeting women at a restaurant in Riverdale, and soliciting prostitutes, were all secondhand? Anything that came from the FBI—their saying, for example,

*that the wife of a California dentist was his mistress—was
tainted, given their campaign to discredit him at any cost, first
as a Communist, then later as a lecher. In the public's eyes,
however, accusation was equivalent to proof. His wife dismissed them. He could not. They forced him to reconsider the
vows he'd taken when he was nineteen. He was by no means
an ethical relativist. Indeed, the very thought of that angered
him. But maybe—just maybe—what he preached to others was
impossible. Surely the commandments applied to him as a
Christian minister. It would always be that way. The non-
believer might not be judged or condemned or hurled into
hell, but those who took spiritual vows—and them only—were
subject to the narrow system, the "razor's edge," as some called
it, of punishment and redemption. Consequence was reserved
only for spiritual aspirants. These could not afford the slightest
hint of moral failure, not a moment of weakness lest that be
used against their cause. How did the old churchwomen put
it? Dirt shows the quickest on the cleanest cotton. And if nothing could be found, they would have to live with misdeeds
fabricated and passed along to reporters who received "information" on him from the government's Crime Records Division. And in the horrible tape of a party in his hotel room,
which his wife found at the SCLC's office, mailed by a Bureau
agent in November of 1964 from Miami, just thirty-four days
before he was to accept the Nobel Prize for Peace. He'd been at
that raucous party, yes. People there told dirty jokes. A listener
could conclude there was sexual activity in the room, but
nothing—absolutely nothing—on the tape directly implicated
him. His voice could barely be heard in the room. So Hoover
ordered his lab to enhance his words a little, and when the
supposedly damaging tape reached his wife it came with a letter that said: "Look into your heart. You know you are a complete fraud and a great liability to all of us Negroes . . . You
could have been our greatest leader . . . But you are done . . .*

There is but one way out for you. You better take it before your filthy, abnormal fraudulent self is bared to the nation."

Many nights when he lay beside his wife, unable to sleep, he did want to put a gun to his head. To his congregation he'd said, "There is a Mr. Hyde and Dr. Jekyll in us," and not once did he exclude himself from the realm of sinners, though more than anything else in this world he wanted to be a good man.

One thing—one poem—often steadied him during these nights of despair, lines composed four centuries earlier by his (and his father's) namesake, Martin Luther:

> This life, therefore
> is not righteousness
> but growth in righteousness
> not health but healing
> not being but becoming
> not rest but exercise.
>
> We are not yet what we shall be
> but we are growing toward it.
> The process is not yet finished
> but it is going on,
> this is not the end
> but it is the road.
>
> All does not gleam in glory
> but all is being purified.

Dexter cracked open his workroom door, holding a football. "Daddy, I'm sorry. I thought you were done working."

"I am, but I'm finished," he said. "At least for now."

His son crossed the room, grabbing two of his fingers, and began pulling him outside toward the living room to play. He knew he would give his children this time, regardless of whether they kept him away from his work all evening. They were the Lord's children, after all, and just as he was the chan-

nel for the gospel and not its source, he and his wife were merely the children's temporary custodians. He knew he had let them down time and again. But Scripture said if a man tried—and kept trying—to serve the good, the true, and the beautiful, Providence would not turn its back. No man, he knew, was given burdens too great for him to carry; indeed, the point was to pass beyond the vanity that he, not God, bore that burden, and realize, even if he had to learn it the hard way and at almost a fatal price, that the challenge of the spiritual was simply this: to be good, truly moral, and in control of oneself for this moment only, because what other moment in time could a man be held responsible for?

II

"We were pulling for you from the start," said Groat. He sat at the kitchen table, which he and Withersby had covered with weathered, string-tied portfolios crammed with reams of green-tinted paper. It was the first time I'd seen Groat up close and in strong light. A fat, froggish man, he lifted the soft drink I gave him and drained it in one long swallow. His skin had the texture of rice paper. His sweat smelled oily. Clearly, he did not meet the weight standard set for federal agents, which meant either he or his physician falsified his yearly medical examinations in order to save his job. He talked on for a while in his thick-tongued voice about his arthritis, his recurring knee problems, reciting his weaknesses and defects the way people sometimes do to disarm you, as if to say they know full well their deficiencies and need to mention them before you take notice and think poorly of them. On the other hand, I thought, this might be nothing more than a ploy to shape our opinions of him before we'd properly had time to pass judgment.

"Back in Washington," he said, giving his brittle, snaplike smile, "there's a lot of . . . concern . . . about what's happening to Dr. King." Groat lifted a pack of Winstons from his shirt pocket, lit one, blew smoke toward the ceiling, then flicked the ash into his soda can. "His friends, some of his closest aides, are damned worried. Did you two know that?"

"No," I said. "Worried about what?"

"Despair, fits of depression." Groat spread open one of his portfolios, then read from his pages like a doctor delivering a diagnosis, his face knotted around the eyes. "According to reports I've got here, he's got everyone worried. Most of the time he's morose, distracted. Can't sleep at night, so he stays up making his staff listen to his sermons over and over again. I figure he's worn out Andrew Young by now, and earlier this month when he took a vacation—about the first he's had in years—he damned near scared Ralph Abernathy to death after he got out of bed in his pajamas and started singing "Rock of Ages" on his hotel balcony. More people on Atlanta's SCLC staff than I care to mention can't see the logic behind his plan to flood Washington with the poor; he's known to walk out of those meetings when things don't go his way. See, I think it's the strain. All the riots and death in the cities last year. And the years before that. He blames himself for them. And if he doesn't, if he denies that there's blood on his hands, his critics lay the corpses right on his doorstep, telling him the day of nonviolence is done, that it was just a foolish dream anyway. Then you got to figure how he's feeling, what with Adam Clayton Powell calling him Martin Loser King, H. Rap Brown taking over SNCC, donations to the SCLC dropping, and one of his own folks, James Bevel, saying whites are the most savage, bestial, murderous, and corrupt people on earth 'cause at bottom they're mentally ill. Look at all he's got stacked against him. Every civil rights leader—Roy Wilkins, Whitney Young, Jackie Robinson, Ralph Bunche, and even King's own father at first—says his stand against Vietnam is the most reckless thing he's ever done, a move that'll splinter the Movement right down the middle, seeing how the military's been at the forefront of integration, and Johnson's committed himself to the Great Society's war on poverty. His former allies feel betrayed. His enemies constantly tell him he's failed. That's right, he hasn't had a civil rights victory in two years. And it's showing. Hairline cracks here and there, ones he can't hide. He told Jesse Jackson he ought to go on one of those Gandhi-like fasts unto death to make the rioters in the cities stop and the bickering factions among black activists come together. You watch him out in public, you'll see how his eyes keep moving, looking for someone about to attack him. That's called paranoia, isn't it? When he's talking, he balls his right fist and keeps rubbing his fingers with his thumb. His speeches sound morbid. They're all about dying. Hell, you listen close enough, they sound like they're about a death wish. Not long ago he sent his wife a bouquet of plastic flowers. Red carnations. And when she asked him why, he told her, 'I wanted to give you something you could always keep.' Does that sound like a man who has given up or what? Just between you and me, one of his friends has been urging him to see a psychiatrist . . ."

Withersby rubbed his nose, looking up from his notepad. "He shot that idea down. I think he's suspicious of psycho-analysis."

"Comes from his college days," Groat agreed. "He's probably worried some shrink'll go right to those two times he tried to commit suicide when he was a kid."

"Yes, but look at Malcolm Little. He was better on that

score." Withersby glanced from Groat to me, then to Smith. "During the last year of his life, before those Muslims shot him onstage at the Audubon Ballroom, he was looking into analysis to understand how for seven years he could have preached that doctrine of Yacub, the black scientist, being the inventor of the white race. He told photographer Gordon Parks he'd been mad and sick earlier. Actually, what he said—I've got the report right here—was, 'I was a zombie—like all the rest of them. I was hypnotized, pointed in a certain direction and told to march.'"

Groat rocked his head. "I read that report. It's sad it took so long for him to come to his senses. But, you know, I think Little made a lot of sense. I'm all for integration, but you ought to see some of the slime me'n Vincent spend our time investigating, scumbags like Carlo Gambino, the Gallo brothers, and Joe Columbo. I mean, do colored folks really want to integrate with them?"

"Why," Smith asked, "are you telling us this?"

"Because we think you can help King before it's too late. As you can tell, he won't—or can't—slow down. Not even for a day. You know, it's funny how some men try to kill themselves. Not all of them take pills or stick a shotgun in their mouths. Some I've seen force policemen to do it for them. Others, the workaholics, do it slow. They do it by taking on tasks they know they can't finish, projects they know will put them six feet under. I think that's what we've got here. Damn near every hand is turned against this man. And what does he do? Plan night and day to bring all the poor together in April to disrupt and shut down the federal government, despite his pal Rustin telling him there's no way he's gonna get Irishmen, Puerto Ricans, Indians, Chicanos, and Negroes to put aside their differences and form an alliance. He brought some of their leaders together a few weeks ago, and what they said was, 'Our problems are different from yours.' A sane man might have second thoughts, he might wonder if he's over-reaching himself, especially since his antiwar work's depleted most of his funds. He'd probably wonder, I'm saying, if this last, greatest dream of his—this jump from race to class, from local crises to a national one—might turn into a nightmare when he brings all those poor people to Washington to demonstrate and fill up the hospitals and jails. He'd ask himself, What if there's violence? How do we feed them? Where will they sleep? Or go to the toilet? Now me, I believe in what he used to stand for. I'm a Democrat, I voted for Kennedy. King's done some good work, but there's a problem. It's the company he keeps. Ex-Communists and fellow travelers. In Washington they figure if he's not red, he's awfully doggone pink. Maybe a security risk. And dammit, I think they're right. He's calling for an Economic Bill of Rights, the redistribution of wealth, and a guaranteed income. Listen to this note King made to himself in fifty-one. 'It is a well-known fact that no social institution can survive when it has outlived its usefulness. This capitalism has done. It has failed to meet the needs of the masses.' Now, that sure as hell sounds to me like what I hear coming from behind the Iron Curtain. What do you think?"

Smith and I did not say.

"Thing is, me'n Vincent can't figure how he can be so red when Daddy King is a capitalist. And what about that fellah A. G. Gaston, the black insurance man who paid five thousand to bail King out of jail in Birmingham? Gaston's worth ten mil. He says the *Wall Street Journal* is his Bible, and he published a book called *Green Power,* arguing that money was the key to solving the race problem. You'd think the Reverend woulda noticed how even he depended on creative free enterprise, right?"

"What in God's name"—Smith squinted at Groat—"do you people want?"

"A li'l cooperation," said Groat. "For Dr. King's sake. Anybody can see he's over the edge. The seeds were in his personality from the beginning. A domineering father. Guilt feelings from his privileged status as a famous preacher's son. The sense that he had a racial mission—a destiny—to fulfill, that he was personally responsible for eliminating the world's suffering. Messiah complex. Maybe his being so short figures in too. And there's hypersensitivity to how others saw him, like at Crozer when he overdressed and wouldn't go to class unless his clothes were immaculately pressed, his shoes perfectly shined, and he was, he says, morbidly conscious of being a minute late because he felt any lapse in perfection confirmed negative Negro stereotypes. He never fails to check the polls ranking colored leaders to make sure he's there, preferably in first place. We're talking about an Alpha male determined to leave his mark on the world, even if it's a burn mark from scorching a city. Somebody who'd sacrifice children, for God's sake, on the front lines of a demonstration in order to impose his will on a community. This country deserves a better—a more balanced—black leader than that. Somebody responsible, like Roy Wilkins or that attorney Samuel R. Pierce Jr. Did you see the *Time* article on King when they selected him as Man of the Year? If you haven't, you might want to read that. They point out how Wilkins is sharper than King, he's a better organizer at the NAACP, and that's one of the minister's worst problems—organization—which is why he has to keep an old homosexual red like Rustin around. James Farmer at CORE, they said, is more militant, SNCC's leader John Lewis has King beat for militancy, Whitney Young Jr.'s got it all over him for sophistication, and he'll never write a line that'd stand beside James Baldwin's prose. Right about now, I'd say, he's more of a liability to the civil rights movement than an asset. Truth is, I figure he's even dangerous to himself. Now, that wasn't always so. Once upon a time he was a damned good leader. Do you remember that talk he gave on some things colored people should do, oh, back in fifty-eight, I believe. I've got a copy of it right here."

"We don't need to see that," Smith said.

And we didn't.

I remembered it only too well. Few people talked these days about that speech delivered at the Holt Street Baptist Church for the MIA's Institute on Non-Violence. It had brought the young King great criticism from the black world. He'd said the unspeakable; he'd aired "dirty laundry" and risked, some said, giving ammunition—aid and comfort—to the Movement's enemies. His intent, of course, had been otherwise. It had been to chase down truth, as he'd always tried to do. The things he assailed that night were, in his view, the products of racism, but that did not mean they could be excused or ignored. Preparing for his trip to India, he asked the gathering at the Holt Street Baptist Church to consider—just consider—the arguments of their worst foes, as Gandhi did those of his adversaries, and if their charges contained any truth, then he urged black people to make sure the race was "ready for integration." Their enemies in the South said all that Negroes wanted was to marry white women. He dismissed that lunacy with a wave of his hand but then added, "They say that we smell. Well, the fact is some of us do smell. I know most Negroes do not have money to fly to Paris and buy enticing perfumes, but no one is so poor that he can't buy a five-cent bar of soap." Then he let go, allowing his blistering sermon to take him where it would, to the things internal to the race that hurt and infuriated him. "We kill each other and cut each other too much!" Our crime and illegitimacy rates, he said, are disproportionately high compared with those of whites. No one, King roared that night, needed to speak good English in order to be good; however, that didn't excuse schoolteachers who crippled their students with bad grammar. He moved on that evening from target to target, aiming at alcoholism ("The money Negroes spend on liquor in Alabama in one year is enough to endow three or four colleges"); at the conspicuous consumption some blacks saw as "style" ("There are too many Negroes with $2,000 incomes riding around in $5,000 cars"); and even at black physicians more concerned with status symbols than with deepening their knowledge ("Too many Negro doctors have not opened a book since leaving medical school"). Sometimes, he implied, we need to think less about what we should do and more about what we should be. Changing this litany of inherently moral problems, which could not be ignored—and might worsen over time and even threaten the Movement's progress—was, King said, something within black America's power then, irrespective of what the federal government did or did not do.

His 1958 sermon had been worthy of Booker T. Washington, Marcus Garvey, or Elijah Muhammad (at his best). Sadly, it brought less praise than scathing condemnation from many black people who called him an Uncle Tom. Understandably, the minister gave fewer and fewer of those speeches after the 1950s, though it was this side of King, I realized, that interested these Wise Guys most.

But Wilkins as a potential replacement? That made sense, I supposed. The executive director of the NAACP deeply envied King, often called him a liar, and met with the Bureau's Cartha DeLoach to discuss their mutual dissatisfaction with King; Wilkins worried that the minister's escalating conflicts with Hoover, and King damning the FBI for not protecting civil rights workers, would severely impair the Movement's progress. In fact, Wilkins along with a few other Negro leaders led the effort three years earlier to get King to accept the presidency of a small college or the position of pastor at a large black church in order to retire him as the foremost Negro leader. No, there was no love lost between Wilkins and King, who'd refused the executive director's offer by saying he knew only too well "the hypocrisy of adulation."

"What," I asked, "do you want with us?"

"Like I said, a li'l cooperation. But you don't have to do a thing, Matthew. You can rest." He fanned himself with one of his folders. "We know how well you and the Griffith girl brought along Chaym. Know a li'l about his history too. His kin's from down here originally. On his mother's side, we can trace his family tree back to a free woman named Baleka Calhoun. She came over in a slave ship before Surrender. Belonged to an African tribe called the Allmuseri. They're all dead now, of course, or moved on. He's pretty much the last of his line. Now, what I been thinking is if Zorro—"

"Who?" I said.

A quick, elastic little grin quivered round Groat's mouth. "Excuse me, I meant to say if *Dr. King* was to one day lose his standing as a leader, he'd have to retire, now wouldn't he? And it'd probably be the best thing for him, and for the country—if we saved him from himself, I mean."

I asked, "How could that happen?"

"It's something we'd like to discuss with Chaym . . . alone, if you wouldn't mind."

"I think you'd better leave now," said Smith. "I'm not interested in anything you have to say."

Groat chuckled and gave Withersby a sideways glance. "We'll leave, if that's what you want. But I just want to say that it'd be a shame if somebody decided to reopen the investigation into who killed Juanita Lomax and her kids."

Withersby added, "Don't forget that apartment fire on Indiana Avenue."

"Oh, that's right! Whoever did that would be facing, oh, what would you say, Vincent?"

"Twenty years, easy."

Groat gave a headshake and scratched his chin. "Mm-hmm. I'd say that."

Smith looked as if his mind had stopped. The line of his lips thickened. When he spoke, his voice shook. "Listen, I was just starting to put my life back together. Right here, in this place—"

"That's good to hear," said Groat. "It's something you could come back to, and with a whole lot more money to help you make it better. Do you think we could take a ride and talk a little more?"

"Do I have a choice?"

"Not really."

"Chaym," I said, "you can't go with them—"

"Matthew." Withersby looked square at me. "This doesn't concern you anymore. The best thing for you to do is go back to Chicago. Maybe get back in school. Or maybe you'd like to think about becoming an agent. I believe you'd be a good one. I could help you with your application, if you like."

"No, thank you."

Smith looked at me as a man might if a noose was tied round his neck. "It's all right, we're just gonna talk." Then he laughed, brokenly. "It's just a li'l karma catching up with me, I guess. Check your Deuteronomy 32:35."

I followed them to the front door, coming close up behind the Wise Guys just in time to hear Smith asking a question that had bothered me from the beginning. "How long have you been watching us?"

"Since the day you arrived at King's apartment," Withersby said. "You know, it's a shame someone as talented as you has always been in the shadows. But that happens to geniuses, doesn't it?"

"You think that's what I am?"

"I know it, Chaym. And we want to help you . . ."

After they left, squeezing Smith between them on the front seat of their green Plymouth, pulling away at twilight, I sat on the front porch for hours, drinking a six-pack of Budweiser, waiting for them to return. In the distance, darkness began to stain the horizon, the hills, all the farmhouses, and the blue silhouettes of trees were black against the sky. Then it was night, and the world shrank. Was smaller, it seemed to me. Each time I saw a pair of headlights appear on the narrow, root-covered road, I stepped drunkenly into the yard, straining my eyes, only to see those lights pass the farmhouse by. I returned to the porch, starting on a second six-pack. And waited. The more I drank, the more the palpable dread I felt mercifully dulled, but I was unable to shake off Withersby's words and wanted to shoot him. There was something awful in the way he'd said it, *We want to help you,* as if he knew well the demons of desire and inadequacy that dwelled within Smith, all those decades of never being appreciated, and was playing him, but for what?

What possible use could these Wise Guys have for the minister's double? I tore the tab off another beer, drained half its contents, and belched, remembering that leaders like Hitler and Stalin employed stand-ins, and it was rumored that Fidel Castro had a couple of look-alike actors always waiting in the wings to impersonate him. So we had envisioned Smith's role from the start. But what happened to doubles when the original became expendable, or a liability? I wondered: What if the Wise Guys really had no use for him? No more than they did for King. What if their assignment was to eliminate or discredit the minister—wouldn't they want to eliminate as well the one capable of standing in during his absence?

By midnight they still had not returned. My stomach felt sour. My thoughts kept twisting, torquing so I could not stay any longer on the porch, listening to the wind whirling leaves and whistling in the treetops. I went inside the empty farm-house, which seemed desolate and ghostlike, now that Amy was gone for good and, I feared, Smith was gone too. My aimless pacing took me through the front room where he'd devoted himself to studying minutiae of the minister's life, to the spot in the kitchen where I'd kissed Amy, and finally to the closed door of Smith's bedroom. I turned the knob, cracking open the door. I stepped inside, clicked on the ceiling light, and sat heavily down on his bed. There in one corner was his dented saxophone. I picked it up, plopped down again on the bed, wet the mouthpiece, and tried to play, producing not the mellow sound he'd conjured from his instrument but instead a *blaat!* that more resembled breaking wind than melody. No, I would never be a musician.

I returned the horn to its place in the corner, and as I turned around I saw something sticking out from under his bed, barely concealed by the blanket. I got down on one knee, peered under the mattress, and found a cardboard box filled with sketches, some in watercolor, others in charcoal. I spread them on the bed. It had been months since I'd seen his drawings, months in which his heart had subtly begun to change. His earlier pieces, I recalled, had seemed anguished and grotesque, some indebted to George Grosz's savage depictions of the German bourgeoisie during World War II, except that earlier Smith's targets were Negroes and American whites who betrayed the dream of the beloved community—race merchants who capitalized on their people's suffering for personal profit, black thieves who preyed upon the poor unable to escape them in an era of apartheid, and Caucasians so guilt-ridden by the sins of their forebears they lost all reason when blackmailing, professional Race Men accused them of every social crime imaginable; all these players fell beneath Smith's brutal pen and brushwork, the opportunists, race pimps and profiteers, and bigots whom he always drew dragging their knuckles on the ground like Neanderthals. But these new pages he'd filled, showing them to no one, shoving them under his bed in a cardboard box, were astonishingly different. In some way he'd descended into hell in his earlier work, during his days of exile, facing without flinching the ugliest, most paralyzing features of color and caste and inequality, squeezing them for every drop of pus and corruption they contained. And then, sometime after taking the bullet intended for King (so the dates on his drawings suggested), he'd let that go, released it. His new sketches were simplicity itself: delicate, lovingly detailed studies of the landscape around the farmhouse in different gradations of light. There were at least two dozen wordless meditations on a single ramose tree in the front yard, as if that one object—seen clearly and through no eyes but his own—might reveal the world's mystery and wonder. He reveled in the play of colors, knowing they did not exist—colors, secondary qualities—outside the miracle of consciousness, which made every one of us (so his notebooks claimed) the magister ludi, the maestro of each moment of perception. I found drawings of Amy so real, so naturalistically rendered, it seemed she had appeared instantaneously, transported from Chicago to Carbondale like the spacemen in a TV series. There were several portraits of me, though I barely recognized myself. Me as he envisioned I might be in a decade, no longer the insecure, callow prop in the background of someone else's story (or the chronicles of a mass movement) but instead an individual inexhaustible and ineffable in his haecceitas and open-ended promise. I stared and stared at these portraits. I went through all his sketches, studying each carefully, and I came to see that in them Smith had decided that if the world our absent fathers made was hideous, unfair, and unacceptable, a realm where we were condemned, then all right: he would reinvent it from scratch, if need be, in his art and actions.

His notebooks were no less revealing, the yellowed pages bearing his minute transcriptions of verse by Shinkichi Takahasi:

> The wind blows hard among the pines
> Toward the beginning
> Of an endless past.
> Listen: you've heard everything.

And from Shinsho:

> Does one really have to fret
> About Enlightenment?
> No matter what road I travel,
> I'm going home.

It was dawn before I finished reviewing his sketches and notebooks, and still the green Plymouth had not returned. Exhausted, I fell asleep on his bed, surrounded by drawings, and didn't wake until late afternoon. I stumbled to the front porch: nothing. No one. And then I began to suspect they had killed him. All day long I watched the road, emptied every bottle and beer can in the kitchen, and turned to the spiral-bound college notebook in which I kept a record of our covert project for the Revolution, catching up on my entries, trying to describe everything I remembered since the Wise Guys intervened with as much accuracy as I could muster, though even as I wrote and drank I heard Smith's caveat that words always disguised as much as they delivered, covered up as much as they clarified, and by twilight I doubted every event and experience I'd squeezed into that ontological unit, the Procrustean bed of the English sentence. Come evening, I could stay at the Nest no longer. I climbed in the Chevelle and rode aimlessly for half an hour on the hills and backroads of Little Egypt, driving with my elbow out of the window, fingers curled on the roof. I stopped at a filling station, bought a newspaper, and read of a disaster in Memphis during a demonstration for striking sanitation workers. Sixty people injured. A sixteen-year-old black boy shot in the back. One hundred fifty-five stores damaged. I tossed the paper on the backseat, climbed behind the wheel, and drove for another hour until I realized my directionless wandering had brought me to Rev. Littlewood's church.

It was beginning to rain. The air was cool, turning to chill. A few fireflies drifted by. From the outside, Bethel was quiet as a tomb. There were no services on weekday evenings. I let myself in, soaking wet, switched on the lights, and immediately the sedate ambience of the church crept into me. Naturally, I first noticed our labor—our lives distilled, a kind of prayer itself—in the repairs to the entryway, pews, balustrades, and pulpit. All of it anonymous, of course. Unsigned. Nevertheless, I knew a twinge of satisfaction as I walked to the front row of benches, my footsteps echoing loudly; then I sat down and dripped. Wind battered the high stained-glass windows. Rain drummed on the roof. I looked at the new doors we'd installed on either side of the stage, and then my eyes came to rest on the two portraits of Jesus behind the podium. In one an angel comforted him in the Garden of Gethsemane; in the other, Simon the Cyrene, an African, carried to Golgotha the heavy wooden cross to which the bone-weary Nazarene would be nailed by his enemies. In the stillness of Bethel's sanctuary, I found myself falling toward that image, wondering how Simon, a man from the country, felt when the Roman soldiers conscripted him to shoulder the rood: a black man from the most despised tribe on earth given the priceless gift of easing the suffering of a savior. In that scene, he was an extra. On stage for but a sentence in Matthew 27:32. He was given no speech. In Hollywood, he would have been paid the union minimum. Most likely he wouldn't be found in the credits. And after one magnificent moment of serendipity and contingency, of accident and chance (not unlike the young King's being in Montgomery at the right moment to merge with history), Simon blended anonymously—invisibly—back into the wailing crowd. Outside history. I felt I knew him. Was him. No man could equal the Nazarene. But Simon? I was thinking that here was a black man I might measure myself against, a standard I could attain, when behind me I heard a soft-breathing voice, one as firm and deep as an old country well.

"Matthew—"

Startled, I swung my head round and saw the minister sitting behind me. My jaw fell halfway. My breath went out of me. "Sir, I didn't know you were—"

"Uh-uh, it's me, buddy."

"Chaym?"

I knuckled my eyes. I looked again. It *was* Smith, shaven, with his hair cropped short, wearing a blue suit and tie. There was a rain-dampened trenchcoat spread over his knees. He looked more like King than at any time before. "Where have you been?"

"You don't want to know."

"Can I help?"

"I doubt it. Naw, I can't be saved . . ."

"What did they do to you?"

"Just talk. They got me a new place to stay and my wallet's fat."

"You took it?"

"I don't have much choice, do I?" He let his shoulders relax and reached into a pocket of his suitcoat. "Maybe you don't understand. They've got me over a barrel. And I'm scared. I ain't ashamed to say that. The things they're talking about . . . what they want me to do to embarrass him . . . the shit they're up to in Memphis . . . I don't know what I'm gonna do. I don't want to go to prison. I'd die before I'd let anybody lock me up again, but I don't know if I want to live if I do what they're asking." He closed his eyes, pressing the heel of his hand against his forehead. "They're outside in the car. They let me go to the farmhouse to pick up some of my things. When I didn't see you there, I figured maybe you'd be here. I told them I left some of my stuff at Bethel . . ." He withdrew a folded sheet of paper from his coat and handed it to me. "I found one of these. Thought I'd give it to you, just to tidy things up a bit."

I opened the paper. It was the Commitment Blank. The decalogue of the Movement. Which he'd signed.

"Give that to the sister for me, all right?"

"Chaym—"

"It's over, Bishop."

"Wait." I tried to lighten things a little. "I thought you wanted to help with my salvation."

He raised his shoulders in a shrug. "Sorry. You're on your own. But there is one thing you can do for me."

Had it not been for the wink he gave me, I would have thought I was listening and talking to King. How could I refuse him anything? "What?"

"Pray for me. I can't do that for myself."

"Of course. I will, but—"

"Do it *now*."

He waited, fixing me so fiercely with his eyes I turned in my seat, bringing my hands together, the wrinkled Movement decalogue between my fingers. But as before, no words came to me. My faith was frail. Prayers had always failed me. Like millions of black men, I was a bastard who'd never known his father—the word used for people like me was "illegitimate." Whoever my father was, he'd rejected me long ago. How could I pray to a Father? I squeezed my eyes tighter, thinking of Chaym's troubles, and those of the minister. Slowly I petitioned whatever powers that be, regardless of what they thought of me, to keep them from harm, praying not for myself as I'd always done, but instead for those I loved, and as the sense of their fragility and my own filled me, our lives of a few hours in a world of two minutes, the evil that waited outside our door, I felt something slam inside my chest, then hot tears were hopping down my cheeks, and instead of offering words I wept for my counterfeit, fatherless status, gave myself over to it shamelessly, and by the end of my halting, stumbling appeal I felt emptied, no longer trying to bring a distant God's grace to my finite desires as His cast-aside son, but only wishing *Thy will be done.*

I took out my handkerchief, cleaned my spectacles, and blew my nose. I turned in my seat. Smith was gone. The benches behind me, row after row, were unpeopled, and the front door of Bethel AME creaked open onto the unsearchable darkness, as if a djinn had passed into our lives and just as miraculously disappeared.

12

It was the greatest mistake of his life, and he had no one but himself to blame. Sitting with his arms folded across his knees beside an equally baffled and speechless Abernathy in the Rivermont Hotel, he stared, his face squeezed shut, at televised scenes of bloodshed and civil breakdown on the downtown streets of Memphis. He'd been out there just minutes before, leading a crowd of six thousand down Main Street from the Clayborn Temple to protest the city's blatantly racist treatment of black sanitation workers. They'd marched all of three blocks before he heard glass breaking in clothing stores behind him. Turning, he saw black teenagers, some wearing stocking caps to hold their processed hair in place, pillaging shoes and suitcoats priced at $89.95 through plate-glass windows, then the police moving toward them, and he'd cried out, "Stop this, I won't lead a violent march," but it was too late. Evil was free. To save his life aides pulled him into a passing car, sped through the police barricades, and delivered him, not back to the black-owned and -operated Lorraine Motel, but to a deluxe hotel in a white neighborhood overlooking the Mississippi.

"God Almighty, we waltzed right into this one." Abernathy's eyes watered as he watched cops with butchwax crewcuts driving elderly black demonstrators in raincoats from the empty streets onto sidewalks, where they pinned them to the pavement, jamming their knees into the backs of anyone who resisted. "Why the devil didn't somebody do their homework before we got here?"

"Ralph, you've got to get me out of Memphis."

"Soon," Abernathy said. "As soon as we can settle things here."

"I don't think I can take any more—"

"Tomorrow. We've got a flight in the morning."

"Ralph . . ."

"Yes?"

"Am I doing any good?"

"I think you know the answer to that."

"No," he said. "No, I don't."

In the next room the phone was ringing. There was pounding on the hotel's door. From what he could tell, the hallway was filled with people. James Lawson's folks, no doubt. And reporters—they were always at his heels, asking him to comment on everything colored men did on this earth, or analyze every new political development, forever asking him for answers, predictions, opinions. In his youth, right out of B.U., he had four answers for any question the media posed to him. Fifteen years later what he wanted most for himself—for Martin—was a brief withdrawal, a retreat for meditation and reflection. But now they had a bona fide catastrophe, one with his name attached to it. One they could say destroyed his beliefs forever.

Abernathy let his head fall back on the sofa; he stared at the white ceiling. Then, abruptly, he said, "ML, you've got to talk to them."

His insides were shaking. Brackish fluids from his belly kept climbing up his throat, and he kept swallowing to force down the backwash. The room was swimming. It felt wrong, all of it. Outside the window of his two-bedroom suite, in a garden that made him think of Gethsemane, trees were leaved lusciously, the quiet was broken only by songbirds while downtown the police were painting the streets with blood. He clamped shut his eyes. Now he understood the meaning of Paul's words, "I die daily."

"Not now . . ."

"You want me to run interference?"

"Please, I can't see anybody right now." His voice shook. "Buy me some time."

Abernathy gave him a pat on his shoulder, then pulled his suitcoat off the back of the chair, slipped his arms through the sleeves, adjusted his tie, and went to answer the door. Once Abernathy was gone, he threw up on the sofa. Then he put his head in his trembling hands and cried until he felt clean. He'd wept often and easily in 1967, trailing tears across a continent, from Atlanta to Washington, from New York to Marks, Mississippi, where in preparation for the ambitious Poor People's Campaign he'd interviewed black tenant workers with teeth colored like Indian corn. In their tin-roofed shacks he saw barefoot children, their stomachs bloated, wearing clothes woven from dirt: babies living in conditions as miserable as those of the Untouchables in India, but Gandhi had given them a different title, Harijans ("children of God"), and the government officials he and Coretta met were sincere in their commitment to programs aimed at alleviating the suffering of a class it had despised and oppressed for centuries. If there, he wondered, then why not in the wealthiest nation in the world?

217

If America had done so many special things to suppress Negroes, why couldn't it do something special for them? Other ministers, black and white—particularly white ones from rich churches—reminded him that when Jesus was in Bethany at the house of Simon the leper, a woman brought him costly fragrant oil, which set his disciples to complaining, "To what purpose is this waste when the ointment might have been sold for much and given to the poor," and to this Jesus replied, "Ye shall have the poor always with you." Indeed, white preachers cited this often; they were the ones he chastised in his "Letter from Birmingham City Jail," and to them he replied with a passage of his own: "If a man say, I love God, and hateth his brother, he is a liar: for he that loveth not his brother whom he hath seen, how can he love God whom he hath not seen?" But the words of Christ were the horn of his salvation. Poverty would always exist, he knew that. Prejudice, so hydra-headed, could never entirely be eliminated. He knew that too; but no piety from the pages of Scripture could ever justify the fact that the world's suffering poor in the modern era were predominantly black and brown, women and children.

Later that night, as he drank to dull the pain in his mouth (he'd ground down on his teeth and crushed a filling), he watched baton-wielding motorcycle policemen, jackbooted and jacketed, wade into black rioters on Main Street. Three thousand National Guardsmen and a phalanx of olive-green tanks and trucks rumbled like thunder into town, imposing a dusk-to-dawn curfew. Reports coming through the television told of two hundred eighty arrested, sixty-two clubbed and wounded, and one sixteen-year-old boy killed. No matter what anyone said, that death was on his soul. His critics were right—sometimes he was a damned poor organizer. But how could he oversee everything? Be everywhere at once? He felt he was caught in a current sweeping him relentlessly forward, one in which he was drowning, unable to catch his breath or keep his head above water as the waves propelled him help-lessly on like a man hurtling over Niagara Falls. Abernathy ordered from room service but could not get him to touch a thing on the tray. Or speak, for he felt dim in understanding, weak in flesh, and cold in his heart.

He paced the turquoise carpeted floors of their hotel room in his stocking feet, thinking of that dead teenage boy, blowing cigarette smoke, his collar open and sweat-stained, retracing every step that had directed him away from the prodigious work of preparing for the Poor People's Campaign, with its impossible logistics, to leading this tragic march for the sanita-tion workers. At first, their problems with Mayor Henry Loeb seemed peripheral to the Movement and did not draw his attention until the day, February 12, when thirteen hundred black workers went on strike after the city refused to recognize their union and rejected its demands for a ten percent wage increase and benefits. They marched, wearing and carrying signs proclaiming "I AM a Man." Negroes in the Memphis community rallied behind the strikers, who now and then skir-mished with the police. They listened to civil rights leaders at Mason Temple Church urge them not to return to their jobs before their demands were met. Mayor Loeb's response was to dig in, refusing to talk to their representatives, and he promised to fire all the strikers. The city brought forth an injunction to halt demonstrations on the workers' behalf. Local ministers decided there was only one man who could shore up their battle against Loeb, whom blacks had hugely voted against during his campaign for office.

As Abernathy dozed, he went back to the television, turn-ing the volume down low, on his face the flickering television's glow as the full-scale riot raged on. Transfixed, unable to turn away from the violence, he remembered how he'd turned James Lawson's request to address a Memphis rally over and over in his mind. The timing seemed wrong. He was in the midst of raising money for the proposed three-month spring offensive for the poor, an assault that would force Congress to directly confront economic injustice in America and realize a dream long nurtured by predecessors such as A. Philip Randolph. But how could he turn away from this other just cause? These black sanitation workers needed a nationally visible champion. Earlier in the year two black crewmen were crushed in a grisly accident caused by a garbage truck's compressor. In early February sewer workers were sent home for a day because of bad weather, but while whites received a full day's wage, the blacks were only paid for two hours. The injustices in Memphis were clear, for, as Marx might put it, the sanitation workers provided "socially necessary labor" without which the city would smother in its own sludge. Yet despite the value of their work, these men, who tramped every day down hot alleyways with the filth of the affluent packed in plastic tubs on their backs, and swept away rats and maggots and the stench of so-called civilized life so the wealthy could move about in clean homes and bright workplaces—these invisible men in Memphis, whose clothes were perpetually scented with the waste of others, were denied the most basic forms of decency. Their situation perfectly mirrored the point he wanted to drive home with the Poor People's Campaign. One of his aides jokingly remarked that he was always operating two steps ahead of where he actually was. Perhaps, the aide suggested, he needed to get over his inability to say no to anyone in need, a comment he brushed aside, pointing out that his tour of Mississippi would bring him near Memphis, and once there he would carefully test the waters to see how deep he should dive in.

It so happened that the waters in Memphis were pleasantly warm and felt just fine. On March 18, he spoke to an enthusiastic crowd of nearly seventeen thousand that hung on *his every word as he told them to put aside their class differences and join ranks behind the striking garbagemen, whom he called "as significant as the physician, for if he doesn't work, disease is rampant." For every sentence he sang, the crowd sang back, That's right! and Hallelujah! They stamped their feet, they cheered, and he got into the swing of it, strengthened by their energy, at one with their hopes and dreams of dignity. The injunction wouldn't stop them, he said. Nothing would turn them around because they were tired, so tired, from working day and night and never seeing a living wage. Their men were sick of having their manhood denied, their wives and daughters of being domestic servants. The crowd rocked to his preaching that Monday night, roared its approval. And why not? This was Tennessee and he was a son of the South. There were no nationalists here. The Black Power plague hadn't infected Memphis, not like in Chicago. He was home again. He understood these good, Galilean people. He was of them, and they were happily in the palm of his hand, just as in Birmingham and Montgomery. Lord have mercy! This was what he'd needed for so long, and in that giddy, feel-good moment he made them a promise. If they marched together on Friday, if every working man and woman joined in, and the children too, then they would win. And he promised himself he would lead them.*

It should have been a triumphant march, an exuberant overture, or trial run for the Poor People's Campaign. The problems began when his flight from New York to Memphis was late by two hours. The parade started without him. A little before noon Abernathy met him at the airport and hurried him to the Clayborn Temple; then he was rushed by car toward the front of six thousand restless, edgy Tennesseans already on the move. In the backseat, peering out, he realized something was very wrong. This wasn't a line of protesters. It felt more like an

undisciplined mob. Toward its end he saw young people hold-
ing up placards that read "Black Power Is Here." They were
the Invaders, his driver said. None of them cared for his mes-
sage of nonviolence—they were disciples of Stokely and Rap
Brown—and they had threatened to disrupt the march if they
were not included. Fact was, they'd been a problem since the
Memphis strike began. "And you didn't tell me?" he asked,
grabbing the front seat and pulling himself forward, which jos-
tled his driver. Great Peter only knew why they'd held back this
information. He struck the seat and his driver jumped, hunch-
ing his shoulders, bringing the car to a stop. Up ahead, the
police were closing off Main Street. It was too late to turn
back. Whithersoever he went he knew he would find them, the
violent in spirit, the herren-moralists, the Nietzscheans. Turn-
ing the door handle, lifting himself out of the car, he silently
said a prayer, knowing that men of conviction had to act,
though always on the basis of partial information, blindly forg-
ing ahead and hoping for the best. The word for this from time
immemorial, he knew, was faith.

Which lasted all of three blocks, then died in downtown
Memphis. Most of the marchers returned home or to their
churches. But the Invaders, who had used the march as a
cover, fought on, firing at the police, turning over cars, setting
fires and smashing store windows.

He was still watching the news reports when Abernathy
padded sleepily from the bedroom. His friend of sixteen years
plopped down beside him on the sofa, yawning and knuckling
his red-rimmed eyes. Always his nearness was bracing. As
friends they had the habit of each other, like siblings, and he
could talk candidly with him. They complemented and in
many ways completed each other, though he knew that from
their first meeting in Montgomery Abernathy had, in his
own words, burned with envy at his big-city learning and
confidence.

"Do you good to get some sleep, ML," Abernathy said. "Things out there have to settle down sooner or later."

"Maybe they shouldn't."

"What?"

"If we believe in peace, maybe we should get out of the way and let the separatists and segregationists, the Invaders and racists, black anti-Semites and Klansmen, go at each other in a full-scale war." He coughed, his voice slipping a scale. "They're two of a kind. Just different in color. I can't believe they'll ever change. Hate is too easy. Nonviolence as a way of life may be asking too much of people. Maybe it goes against the grain of something tribal in our genes. Or against the ego. Or the carnal mind, which can only perceive in terms of polarities. If I have to choose between seeing men as fallen angels or risen apes, I prefer the former. You know that. But the apes, black and white, are out there. And their goal is to make the world a jungle. I say, let them kill each other and tear it all down, then God-hungry men and women can make a fresh start."

"You don't mean that . . ."

"I do."

"I think you're just tired."

"Yes, I am. And I think it's over, Ralph."

"No, that's just—"

"Let me finish. I'm not saying we haven't accomplished a great deal. We have. But where can I go from here? After this? Can I keep developing? What can I do? God, I haven't read a book in years! These reporters ask me about the Tet offensive, the Middle East, the Kerner Commission report, and I haven't had one blessed hour to study any of it in depth, but I'm expected to keep on giving speeches, so I do, making it up as I go along. That's shallow. It's skating along the surface when I need to go deeper into things. Into myself, if I'm going to give back anything of value. I feel trapped, like I'm stuck in a hole. I remember from Crozer, in a paper I wrote, that's what the word suffering *means in Sanskrit*: Dukkha. 'Duk,' bad, 'kah,' hole." *He let his breath roll out.* "What I'm trying to say is that if every day doesn't add knowledge, wisdom, and the ability to live life and increase our capacity to love, we are already dead. Does that make any sense?"

"Yes, and what I think is you should get some rest."

"I'll sleep here on the sofa. And, Ralph?"

"Yes?"

"Thanks."

It was quarter to four.

Abernathy stood, clicked off the television and then the lights, and, after tossing a blanket over his friend, returned to his own bedroom.

In the darkness, on the stiff cushions of the sofa, he tossed and turned, trying to find a comfortable position that might beckon sleep, grappling with the perennial dilemma of his public ministry, how to end evil without creating evil; then mercifully his eyelids grew heavy. In the region between waking and slumber he relived his trip to Kerala, feeling the heat, and watching the locals hang pots on coconut trees to collect their milk; but the heat fermented the sweet milk, which became so intoxicating that crows sipping from the pots fell drunkenly to the ground and stumbled about cawing at the wrong time of day. For a few moments he dreamed of journeying there again for the rest he needed so badly, and to probe deeper into their concept of Maya—the world as itself a cradle-to-crypt dream, in which all men were caught and only the blessed allowed to awaken. He looked at his watch. Four-fifteen. He sat up slowly, knowing this was all the sleep he would have this night. Knowing he would have to return to Tennessee. To make things right. To undo the damage. The Washington campaign would have to be postponed. In Memphis, nonviolence was being tested—he was on trial. Already he was clear on the new itinerary. Check out of this room.

Call his wife. Hold a press conference. Fly back to Atlanta for a furious week of meticulous preparations, then return to this war-torn city for a second demonstration and, for himself, a fuller, deeper, and more perfectly realized broken heart.

13

On the evening of April 4 (Thursday) one hundred and twenty-five American cities began erupting in flame: a prophet had fallen. Pronounced dead at 7:05 P.M. The electrifying, awful report that a metal-jacketed 30.-06 bullet brought down the man who was the nation's moral conscience, ripping away the right side of his jaw and neck, severing his spine on the second-floor balcony of the Lorraine Motel, spread through this splintered world like a declaration of war. There came a confusion of tongues in a house divided against itself. "Nonviolence is a dead philosophy," proclaimed Floyd McKissick, "and it was not the black people that killed it. It was the white people that killed nonviolence, and the white racists at that." So many agreed with McKissick. "Get your gun," shouted Stokely Carmichael. "When white America killed Dr. King, she declared war on us!" The rioting and looting that Citizen King had loathed lasted for ten days in a blood-drenched decade that left everyone perpetually short of breath. In Texas, white students cheered when they heard he was dead. (I am not ashamed to say I hated them.) In Washington, D.C., seven hundred blazes blackened the sky. Tendrils of smoke drifted through windows in the White House, where Lyndon Johnson designated Sunday, April 7, a day of national mourning. Flags were lowered to half-staff. Schools closed. The baseball season was postponed. Three networks broadcast his funeral for six hours. Docks were shut down. Pope Paul VI cried out that this "cowardly and atrocious" killing of our better brother "weighed on the conscience of mankind." It was four and a half years since JFK's murder. Four years since Malcolm X's. Robert Kennedy (only two months away from the bullet that would end his life in Los Angeles) had three extra telephones installed in Coretta's home and chartered an Electra jet to bring the body of Atlanta's finest son— now dwelling in a house not made with hands, eternal in the heavens—home to lie in state in the Sisters' Chapel of Spelman College. We had never, I knew, been equal to him, or to the transcendent tasks he called us to perform. He was destined for vaticide. Before this ritualistic blood ceremony, this foundation sacrifice, ended, forty-six people were dead. Whites, pulled from their cars, were beaten mercilessly and stabbed. Two thousand six hundred people were injured. Another twenty-one thousand were arrested, myself and Amy among them at an April 5 demonstration in Chicago, where I'd returned to school.

By Tuesday of that longest week in modern history, I stood in sweltering heat outside Ebenezer Baptist Church in Atlanta, travel-worn and with a bad case of trench mouth. The corners of my eyes were crusted after the long drive from Illinois. My hair was uncombed and dry, the scent in my clothes was the aroma of sweat commingled with fried chicken eaten on the road. My mind felt like a freshly opened grave. I was one of sixty thousand people encircling the building where King was baptized and raised, listening, on a sun-heavy street beneath a cerulean sky, to Dr. L. Harold DeWolf and Rev. Ralph Abernathy on a loudspeaker because we—Amy, Mama Pearl, and myself—were unable to get inside, where nearly eight hundred mourners filled the pews. These, of course, were the dignitaries: Carmichael, who came with his bodyguards, entertainers like Harry Belafonte, Sammy Davis Jr., and Dick Gregory, all of whom had marched arm-in-arm with King. (Marlon Brando pledged ten percent of his earnings to the Cause.) The politicians were there too, particularly the ones running for president that fall (Eugene McCarthy and Richard Nixon, but Hubert Humphrey came instead of LBJ), and we saw the nation's other grand woman of sorrows, Jacqueline Kennedy, enter the crowded church as well. On and on they came to pay their last respects in public, the hypocrites and true bearers of homage to the colored man who died for our collective racial sins and spiritual failures. I felt no need to be inside with them, but as I listened to Abernathy's eloquent speech, my head felt light. My knees buckled a little. Amy, perspiring on her upper lip, put her arm around my waist to steady me. "Are you going to be okay?" I didn't know the answer to that, or to a thousand other questions that had troubled my sleep since King fell in the crosshairs of that high-powered rifle.

But this much I did know:

The day before he died, the sky above Memphis was turgid, the spring air moistened and charged by electricity from a thunderstorm the night before. As I said, I was back in school, studying Brightman, as he'd asked me to do, but I called his hotel on the evening of the third. The whole city knew where he was staying because his room number had been broadcast on several radio stations. He'd picked the Lorraine Motel to stay at after an article appeared in a Memphis paper criticizing him for running away to the Rivermont after the earlier aborted march down Beale Street (it was Bureau copy, of that I was convinced). When he returned to Memphis, detectives assigned to protect him met King at the airport but left after someone in his entourage shouted, "We don't want you here." Local organizers hurried him off to the Lorraine, lodgings that one of his aides, Hosea Williams, found confusing, since they had never stayed there before. He was originally given a room (306) on the ground floor, then reassigned to the second floor (305), and Abernathy was put in the first room. I reached him at about 4 P.M. Tired, he said all he wanted to do that evening was rest before spending most of the next day with organizers for the march. He'd toyed with the idea of finding someone to substitute for him at a rally he was slated to attend at the Mason Temple, and in the end decided to let Abernathy do it for him.

But when Abernathy reached the Mason Temple he found the crowd clamoring for King. That night they would accept no stand-ins. Wearily, the minister changed out of his pajamas and was driven to the temple in pounding rain with Andrew Young and Jesse Jackson (wearing bluejeans and a brown jacket). Without a text, he thundered oratory that made the audience forget the storm lashing the temple's windows. "I want you to know tonight that we as a people will get to the Promised Land," he said. "I'm so happy tonight. I'm not worried about anything. I'm not fearing any man. Mine eyes have seen the glory of the coming of the Lord. I have a dream this afternoon that the brotherhood of man will become a reality . . . With this faith we will be able to achieve this new day, when all God's children—black men and white men, Jews and Gentiles, Protestants and Catholics—will be able to join hands and sing with the Negroes in the spiritual of old. 'Free at last! Free at last! Thank God Almighty we are free at last!'" And when he was done, and turned away from the bank of gleaming microphones, it seemed he fell, exhausted, toward Abernathy, who rushed with outthrown arms to embrace and steady him on his feet.

He and his staff decided to postpone the march for the sanitation workers until Monday. His plan that Wednesday was to visit Rev. Samuel Kyles's home for dinner on Thursday evening. Somewhere I'd heard that on the third he'd dined on catfish, buttered black-eyed peas, and a tossed salad at the Four Way Grill. He asked me, "How is Chaym? The last time we talked, you said you hadn't seen him, that two men came by the farmhouse . . ."

"Yes," I said. "That's right. It's been weeks."

"Do you think those government men killed him?"

"Honestly, I don't know, sir." And I did not. All that was left of Chaym Smith were a few of his deeds and products: paintings, sketchbooks, and his saxophone, which I was learning to play by paying for private lessons with a graduate student in Columbia College's Music Department. Sometimes I sat doing meditation "with seed," as it was called, journeying through passages I'd committed to memory from the spiritual traditions of the world. Occasionally I volunteered at the poorer churches, temples, synagogues, and mosques, though I belonged to none. Now and then when I thought of it, I practiced the Tai Chi Chuan form he'd taught me. And I no longer worried about defining myself or being wrong. "I just pray he's all right."

"So do I. We've had too many casualties already. If it's not Division Five after us, then it's COINTEL-PRO or COMINFIL. Since sixty-three we've had more break-ins than I can remember, and they've planted informants everywhere and . . . Wait, I think someone's calling me—I'd better go."

"Good night," I said, "and God bless you."

"Good-bye, Matthew."

It was the last time we'd spoken. (Why, when he said that, did he sound so like Socrates bidding farewell to Crito?) Later, when I pored over the flood of news reports, trying to make sense of his slaying, my hands shaking, I found only conundrums, as if I was prying open a Chinese puzzle box. The deeper I descended, the funnier-looking these fish appeared. The man in charge of the police and fire departments, I discovered, was Frank Holloman, who'd been with the Bureau for twenty-five years. He and Hoover were friends. In fact, Holloman once ran the Atlanta office of the FBI, which kept the Kings under surveillance. In other words, the Bureau had Memphis locked up tight. Yet King had no security—his own people had run them off because they didn't trust the police. The city had assigned two detectives, one of them a black man named Ed Reddick, to be in Fire Station 2, just south of the Lorraine Motel. It was a good location for keeping an eye on the motel, but on that Wednesday two black firemen—Norvell Wallace and Floyd Newsom—were pulled off the job. People said different things about that, and none of them made sense to me. Someone told the firemen there was a threat made against them (some said this was Reddick), so they were transferred, allegedly for their own safety. (Reddick said he did not have them transferred.) But then, Reddick was pulled away too; a Secret Service man from D.C. met him at the station and said there was a contract out on his life, so they sent him home. Yet—and yet—some Negroes called Detective Reddick a spy who felt that one of the black firemen was a militant sympathetic to the strikers. This welter of conflicting "facts," of so many testimonies that contradicted one another, was dizzying, and I swear I didn't have a cross-eyed guess as to who was telling the truth.

And the facts grew stranger with each new string I

pulled. James Earl Ray, a drifter and escaped convict sentenced in 1960 to twenty years in the Missouri State Penitentiary for armed robbery (aliases: Eric Galt, Harvey Lomeyer, John Willard) with a white Mustang bearing Alabama license plate 1-38993, but no motivation for murdering King, was being hunted as the prime suspect for the shooting. But, I wondered, as any sane man would, if a real assassin might leave behind so many fingerprinted items (shaving cream, clippers, a radio with Ray's prison I.D.) to clearly identify him on the street outside Bessie Brewer's boardinghouse at 4221/2 South Main Street? No, that was more than I could accept. In his FBI wanted poster, in his history, Ray perfectly fit the image of a patsy. Or a fool.

The gun, a 760 Remington Gamemaster, was never swabbed to determine if it had been fired. And the copper-jacketed bullet sent to the FBI didn't match—or so I read—the one extracted from King. That bullet entered his lower jaw and cheek one and a half inches below his mouth, hit the jawbone, reentered above the collarbone, then went down (left) through his neck. It was visible as a node in his left shoulder under the skin. Had he lived, he would have been a vegetable. (And who among us could have beared seeing him that way?) According to the physician who removed the bullet in St. Joseph's Hospital, it was intact, its end flattened out. A whole bullet weighed 150 grams. The one dug out of King was 4.7 grams and 3.0 inches round. But that was not the same bullet that found its way with other evidence to Washington, D.C.

Complicating things further, and giving me more sleepless nights than I cared to count, were the claims of two black witnesses at the Lorraine when King went down, one foot stuck in the railing of the balcony, his shoe off, a cigarette crushed in his hand; they claimed they saw a plume of white smoke rise up from the large, hedgelike bushes at the back of the boardinghouse. One was Solomon Jones, King's driver in the limousine, borrowed from a funeral parlor, which was to take King, musician Ben Branch, and Jackson to Rev. Kyles's home. Jones said he saw a man in those bushes. So did Earl Caldwell, a journalist sent to Memphis (his editor at the *New York Times*, he said, wanted him to "nail" King) who heard the shot, followed by someone yelling, "Get low!" People were ducking everywhere in the courtyard, but Caldwell saw a crouching white figure in the bushes, wearing overalls and looking up at the balcony. All those bushes were cut down on April 5 by the police, who said—and I winced at their words—they needed to clear the area to look for evidence.

Inside Ebenezer Church, a choir began singing the minister's favorite hymns, "When I Survey the Wondrous Cross" and "In Christ There Is No East Nor West." Time stood still. The crowd was quiet, intense. A knot gathered in my throat. (I was thinking how, according to Andrew Young, when King fell on that balcony, Jesse Jackson covered his palms with the minister's blood, wiped them on his sweater; then the next day he flew to Chicago to appear bloodstained before the press, declaring he'd held a dying King in his arms. That was untrue, said Young, and I was haunted by the feeling that this act of theater and falsity, this photo-op, would define the spirit of the black struggle for decades after the minister's demise. Had he not said to Carmichael, "I've been used before"?) Then my heart gave a slight jump when Abernathy played a recording of King's sermon, "The Drum Major Instinct," which the minister had delivered at Ebenezer earlier in the year, on February 4, taking his text from Mark 10:35, where James and John, the sons of Zebedee, approach Jesus with their desire to sit beside him in Glory. King's bronze voice, that startling basso profundo, washed over the crowd in skin-prickling waves and reverberated in the ether.

"There is, deep down within all of us, an instinct. It's a kind of drum major instinct—a desire to be out front, a desire to lead the parade, a desire to be first. And it is something that runs a whole gamut of life . . . We all want to be important, to surpass others, to achieve distinction, to lead the parade. Alfred Adler, the great psychoanalyst, contends that this is the dominant impulse . . . this desire for attention . . . Now in adult life, we still have it, and we really never get by it. We like to do something good. And you know, we liked to be praised for it . . . But there comes a time when the drum major instinct can become destructive. And that's where I want to move now . . . Do you know that a lot of the race problem grows out of the drum major instinct? A need that some people have to feel superior. Nations are caught up with the drum major instinct. I must be first. I must be supreme. Our nation must rule the world . . . but let me rush on to my conclusion, because I want you to see what Jesus was really saying . . . Don't give it up. Keep feeling the need for being important. Keep feeling the need for being first. But I want you to be first in love. I want you to be first in moral excellence. I want you to be first in generosity. That's what I want you to do . . ."

Pallbearers brought out King's bier, loading it onto a flatbed farm wagon pulled by two mules—a striking, martyrial phaeton symbolic of the Poor People's Campaign that consumed King's last days. The funeral bells tanged and the wagon began its long trek halfway across Atlanta to Morehouse College, where Rev. Benjamin Mays would give the eulogy. A slow march. A sorrowful march with the mules chacking beneath a sun that burned mercilessly overhead. We fell in behind fifty thousand mourners following the procession. I heard the clop-clop of the mules' heels on hot concrete. Along the way, spectators crowded the sidewalks, a herd of multicolored humanity guilty of sloth, pride, anger, gluttony, covetousness, envy, lust, and acedia. Some dropped to their knees to pray. In spite of myself, my face broke. Amy took my hand, intertwining her fingers with mine, and I took her grandmama's. Dressed in black, Mama Pearl had to be hot, there on a spring day in Atlanta, with the crush of bodies that closed us in. Her skin was sweat-streaked. She was weeping as we walked, her mouth quivering. I gave her my handkerchief.

"He was a beautiful man. I know he's got his jeweled ring and purple robe. And he liked my rugala." She dabbed at her eyes and handed back my handkerchief, rumpled and moist, and thanked me for it.

"*Sama-sama.*"

"How's that again, Matthew?"

"Nothing. I was just thinking—"

"About who killed Dr. King?" asked Amy.

"No," I said. "I know that."

"Who?"

"We all did."

Amy shot me a look, all irritation, as the throng labored with a cautious tread, one that said she couldn't see herself as responsible. But I saw. I understood. We'd killed him—all of us, black and white—because we didn't listen when he was alive, though this was, of course, the way of things: no prophet was accepted in his own country. Even before his death, we were looking for other, more "radical" black spokesmen. The Way of agapic love, with its bottomless demands, had proven too hard for this nation. Hatred and competition were easier. Exalting the ethnic ego proved far less challenging than King's belief in the beloved community. We loved violence—verbal and physical—too dearly. Our collective spirit, the *Geist* of our era, had slain him as surely as

235

the assassin's bullet that cut him down. We were all Cainites. And deservedly cursed. Did we not kill the best in ourselves when we killed King? Wasn't every murder a suicide as well?

All around us, the crowd of the apostates kept pace behind the wagon, concrescing. Walking on, the air now a bright shimmer, I believed in each of us there was a wound, an emptiness that would not be filled in our lifetime. But we could not stop if we wanted to, or go backward.

Amy pressed a little nearer to me, squeezing my hand. "What do you think he'd want us to do now?"

"Excuse me, keep moving forward. If we stop, we'll fall and be trampled."

"Matthew?"

"Eh?"

Her eyes swung up, searching my face. "What about Chaym? Where do you think he is?"

I dropped my gaze, watching my feet and those of the sinners in front of me. I thought hard. "Everywhere . . ."

That seemed to satisfy her, and she smiled as the crowd of the contrite rolled on like a piece of the sea, both of us but waves blending perfectly with its flow, our fingers interlaced, and perhaps she felt, as I did, that if the prophet King had shown us the depths of living possible for those who loved unconditionally in a less than just universe engraved with inequality, and that only the servants should lead, then Chaym had in his covert passage through our lives let us know that, if one missed the Galilean mark, even the pariahs, the fatherless exiles, might sometimes—and occasionally—doeth well.

Amen.

About the Author

CHARLES JOHNSON was the first black American male since Ralph Ellison to win the National Book Award for fiction, which he received for *Middle Passage*. His fiction has been much anthologized, and he was named in a survey conducted by the University of Southern California as one of the ten best short-story writers in America. A widely published literary critic, philosopher, cartoonist, essayist, screenwriter, and lecturer, he is one of twelve African American authors honored in an international stamp series celebrating great writers of the twentieth century. Johnson's alma mater, Southern Illinois University, administers the Charles Johnson Award for Fiction and Poetry, a nationwide competition inaugurated in 1994 for college students. He is currently the Pollock Professor of English at the University of Washington and lives in Seattle.